COCKTAILS OF THE MOVIES

COCKTAILS OF THE MOVIES

AN ILLUSTRATED GUIDE TO CINEMATIC MIXOLOGY

Will Francis and Stacey Marsh

Prestel

Munich · London · New York

CONTENTS

INTRODUCTION

Hollywood has had a lifelong love affair with cocktails. During the 100 years since the movie industry first became established in a Los Angeles valley, the mixed drink has been a central device in the visual language of film.

Changing with fashion and cultural trends through the ages, it has carried different meanings at different times, nuanced within each narrative and environment. A Martini might serve to show a brutal killer's cold sensuality as he sips it in a quiet moment of indulgent solace while, elsewhere, the iconic drink might suggest a demure heroine's steely determination. This cultural shorthand has embedded itself in some of film's most famous moments, from Rick barking 'Play it, Sam' over champagne cocktails in his Casablanca bar (page 64), to James Bond specifying the shaken ingredients of his now-iconic drink in *Casino Royale* (page 144).

By writing and illustrating this book, we gained a fascinating insight into changing tastes in cocktails over the last century. As you browse these pages you'll notice that the earlier movies almost exclusively feature strong drinks served straight up –

that is, in a tall cocktail glass with no ice – and with little in the way of garnish. As we approach the later decades of the 20th century, more tall and iced drinks appear, with a colourful crescendo in the 1990s when not a single drink featured here is served straight up or without ice.

The story of the cocktail goes back much further than that of cinema. The oldest drinks in this book – Flaming Rum Punch and Eggnog – have been around for as long as rum and brandy themselves. In medieval England a drink called Posset was popular, particularly in winter. It consisted of warm milk curdled with alcoholic beverages such as wine or ale. Over time people added spices, distilled spirits and eggs to create Eggnog. Hot punches became popular in the 1600s and were similar to an ancient Norse drink

Flaming Rum Punch (p. 62) & Egg Nog (p. 60)

called Wassail. Punch is believed to have been brought from India by early trading ships, and its name derives from the Sanskrit word for five – *panch* – referring to the main ingredients of spirit, fruit, water, sugar and spices.

In the 17th century, wine and ale had been consumed as a safe alternative to water for centuries, but in 1688 the newly crowned British monarch William III of Orange banned the importation of French brandy. In 1690 he passed the Distilling Act, which allowed anyone to distil their own spirits without a licence. Four years later, heavier taxes were placed on beer, and so the seeds of England's epidemic of gin addiction were sown. By 1720 there were an estimated 7,000 gin shops in London alone. Pharmacies started to sell bitters – grain alcohol infused with botanicals – which were intended for medicinal use but found to make gins of varying quality more drinkable. This tempering of harsh alcohol was the genesis of what we now know as a cocktail. The earliest known mention of a cocktail appeared at the end of that century. Buried in a satirical piece in a 1798 edition of *The Morning Post and Gazetteer* is a reference to a pub drink of 'gin and bitters', and a cryptic reference to a 'cock-tail (vulgarly called ginger)'.

As the 19th century dawned, the first explicit descriptions of cocktails appeared in American publications. These were sometimes referred to as 'slings', a term still used today and derived from the German word *schlingen*, to gulp. Some 60 years later, the cocktail had become a popular concoction of spirit, bitters and sweetener that came in numerous permutations intended to please the palate, and in 1862 the first book detailing cocktail recipes and preparation was released: Jerry Thomas's *Bartender's Guide*, the subtitle of which was *A Bon Vivant's Companion*. Reading this guide, which is still used by bartenders today, we're reminded that, despite all the technological and cultural advances made since the time of Dickens and Tolstoy, we still cherish a well-made drink, served with style and enjoyed in good company. We are still the same *bon vivants* for whom Mr Thomas penned his *Companion*.

As the 20th century dawned, the nascent film industry blossomed in places as diverse as Paris, Melbourne, London and Pittsburgh. Around 1912, movie studios started to move to Los Angeles to escape lawsuits from Thomas Edison (who owned the majority of motion picture patents) and also because of its abundance of sunlight. Cocktails did feature in some of Charlie Chaplin's silent films of the time, but growing fear of the social ills caused by alcohol was about to put the cocktail's stardom on ice.

You may notice that there are no movies in this book from the years between 1920 and 1933. This is due to the era of Prohibition in America, during which the sale and consumption of alcohol was made illegal in what now seems like a bizarre and ill-judged social experiment. It was widely regarded as a failure, fuelling an unprecedented surge in organized crime and illegal alcohol trading, though it has also been credited with some positive developments, such as the demise of violent, male-dominated 'saloon culture' and the invention of fancy soda drinks and ice creams, which possibly drove the subsequent diner and drive-in boom.

During this period many people still drank, though alcohol was expensive and often poor-quality. Hollywood couldn't portray drinking, so almost all films were 'dry'. It was a bad time for the hospitality industry and many of America's star bartenders emigrated to Europe. Finally, in 1933, the law was repealed. As President Franklin D. Roosevelt announced an initial amendment legalizing moderate-strength ale in early 1933, he famously echoed the nation's sentiments by agreeing, 'I think we could all do with a beer.'

In the years since its repeal, Prohibition has itself become the theme of many vintage bars, where cocktails are served in antique glassware while jazz bands and burlesque acts play to a crowd seeking to relive the romance of clandestine hedonism. The period also makes regular appearances in films, with gangsters and the illegal alcohol trade a prominent theme. In *The Great Gatsby*, our only movie here set during the period (page 72), Jay Gatsby enjoys his Highballs with his friend Meyer Wolfsheim in an opulent speakeasy disguised as a Manhattan barbershop. F. Scott Fitzgerald allegedly based this character on Arnold Rothstein, an infamous New York racketeer and one of the first people to profit from the new law – which he did by smuggling in booze from outside the US.

In the three decades that followed, America's drinking culture bounced back with a vengeance, and the art of mixology became something every sophisticate yearned to master. Some of the finest books on the matter were published at this time. Films were awash with drinks and a larger book of this kind could easily focus purely on that era and still leave many unmentioned. It is then that the cocktail really became a star of the silver screen and a pop culture icon in its own right. What ensued was the mass popularization of cocktails. Every bar and restaurant traded on this and their menus were adapted to cater for more mainstream tastes. The first chain bars such as Trader Vic's opened around the world, introducing us to colourful and fruity tiki-style drinks, as seen throughout Elvis Presley's 1961 movie *Blue Hawaii* (page 80). Cocktails became increasingly kitsch, as did the paraphernalia that filled our homes. Search an online auction site for 'vintage cocktail' to see the vestiges – shakers, glassware, furniture, artwork – of a mid-20th-century madness for mixology.

As seems to happen with trends of all types, we are now coming full circle and seeing a huge resurgence of vintage cocktails, with bartenders looking to the early days of mixed drinks once again for inspiration. This is partly due to a general trend for vintage styling in bars and restaurants – from Victorian to mid-20th century – but also, no doubt, because out-of-print mixology guides from days of yore are once again becoming available through small and print on demand publishers. Consequently there is a renewed focus on traditional preparation methods, well-sourced ingredients and drinks that necessitate acquired tastes.

The Old Fashioned, for instance, had become an obscure vintage cocktail until relatively recently, when renewed interest in the early days of mixology coincided perfectly with the drink's appearance as Don Draper's preferred tipple in AMC's television drama *Mad Men*, set in 1960s New York. The drink is once again highly popular, bestowing upon those who drink it an air of urbane sophistication. Equally, the Cosmopolitan was just another colourful cocktail from the 1980s, but once Carrie and friends started to drink

it prominently in the *Sex and the City* TV series and movies, the drink rapidly became a modern classic.

Cocktails of the Movies is structured in such a way as to encourage chance encounters with drinks you may not have previously considered. It is simply ordered alphabetically by cocktail, without sections or chapters. We've aimed to keep the vast majority of recipes easy to make, with the basic ingredients recommended in the next few pages. With a simply stocked cocktail cabinet, you can enjoy creating a surprisingly long list of mixed drinks, entertaining friends and learning about the art of mixology in the process. As David A. Embury reassured readers of his seminal guide *The Fine Art of Mixing Drinks*, first published in 1948, 'anyone can make good cocktails.' It is within easy reach of every reader of this book to become a connoisseur of fine drinking, and the rewards are infinite as you delve into a world where there are countless flavour combinations with which to experiment.

Embury went on to remind those readers who may have been exposed to cocktail snobbery and dogmatism that there really is no perfect or 'right' way to make a cocktail, but that 'the ideal proportions of any drink are those that best suit your particular taste.' So mix with confidence, have fun and feel free to experiment with your own variations on our recipes. We hope these pages provide you with a more interesting way to choose your next cocktail, while in the process learning something new about film and mixology.

Old Fashioned (p. 104)

GETTING
STARTED

TOOLS OF THE TRADE

EVERYTHING YOU NEED TO BECOME A STAR AT THE BAR

SHAKER

Choose between the Boston and Cobbler shaker. The former is simply a large, sturdy glass with a slightly larger steel cup. The latter is a three-piece cup, lid and strainer assembly which, while popular in home bars due to its aesthetic appeal, is in fact less practical and unpopular with professional bartenders. We recommend a Boston set as it is easier to clean, quicker to use and handy for stirred cocktails too.

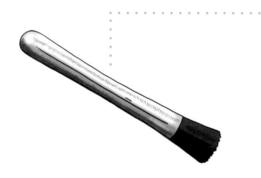

MUDDLER

Fruit and herbs often need to be muddled with sugar or liqueur in the bottom of your mixing glass to release their juices, oils and flavours. Use an unvarnished wooden muddler for gently pressing mint and similar leaves. A steel muddler with raised teeth at one end is best for muddling fruit. Take care not to over-muddle your ingredients as this can leave your cocktail tasting bitter, as well as filling it with a multitude of annoying 'bits'.

BAR SPOON

The unsung hero of the mixologist's toolkit: the traditional bar spoon. With its long, twisted stem joining a flat disc at one end with a large teaspoon at the other, it is indispensable for stirring Old Fashioneds, layering White Russians, measuring syrups, scooping Maraschino cherries from jars and generally making life easier for every bartender. Its flat end can even be used to muddle, though you will find this much easier with the aforementioned muddler.

The greatest achievements come through simple means, and cocktails are no exception. To create fine cocktails at home you really only need a few good-quality tools, which are easily obtainable online or from specialist shops.

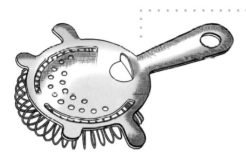

HAWTHORN STRAINER

An essential item if you're using a Boston shaker set. The Hawthorn strainer is the flat, perforated steel paddle with a wire spring around its edge which fits the end of your Boston tin, keeping fruit pieces and ice in while you pour your shaken or stirred cocktail out. It lets out smaller ice shards that have broken up during shaking, as well as some fruit pulp, which is fine for most cocktails served over ice.

FINE STRAINER

For Martinis and the like, which are served without ice in a chilled glass, you'll need to fine strain to avoid fruit pulp and small ice fragments collecting on the surface and spoiling the elegance of your carefully crafted drink. A good fine strainer keeps all these bits out while not getting so clogged up that it stops the drink flowing through into your serving glass.

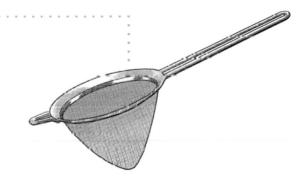

JIGGER

Measuring your cocktail ingredients accurately is crucial not just for making great drinks, but for testing new recipes, refining them and creating your own. A standard steel jigger holds 25 ml in the small end and 50 ml in the large, which translates to one and two shots respectively. The recipes in this book are given in both ounces (oz) and ml. While a fluid ounce is 29.6 ml, you should measure each ounce as one shot; that is, the small end of your jigger filled to the brim.

BASE SPIRITS

THE LEADING LIGHTS OF YOUR COCKTAIL CABINET

GIN

Arguably the most important spirit in your cocktail cabinet, and in the history of mixed drinks, gin is the star of many classics from sweet Martinis to bitter Negronis. To make it, grain alcohol is distilled with botanicals including the traditional juniper berry, together with anything from orange peel to cinnamon to cucumber, to create a unique flavour profile. London gin is dry, while the less common Old Tom gin is sweet. Sloe gin is a berry liqueur made with gin.

WHISKY

Whisky has arguably become a family of spirits, with Scotch, Irish, bourbon and rye the most popular members. They are all distilled from grain mash and aged in wooden casks, with locally available grains and wood determining their distinct flavours. Generally speaking, Scotch whisky is made with peat-smoked malt, Irish with unpeated malt, bourbon with corn (maize) and rye with rye. All must meet minimum cask-ageing requirements if they are legally to bear their name.

VODKA

By far the most neutral spirit, vodka is almost solely pure alcohol (ethanol) and water. It is distilled from starchy foods such as oats, rye, barley, wheat and potatoes. Given vodka's lack of flavour, it is highly useful for giving a kick to already-rich flavour combinations without interfering with the taste. You can even make your own gin by infusing a good vodka with your own blend of botanicals.

The majority of cocktails you will find in this book are made with these six base spirits. When selecting a brand to buy, simply choose the best you can afford, and try something different each time to learn the subtle differences in flavour between one brand and another.

BRANDY

Made from distilled wine, brandy is often drunk on its own and is best consumed at room temperature or slightly warm. It works particularly well in hot cocktails and desserts, to which it adds a beautifully rounded warmth. The most common variety is cognac, which must be from the wine-producing area around the town of the same name, twice-distilled in copper pot stills and aged for two years in special French oak barrels.

RUM

Distilled from molasses, a by-product of refined sugar, most rums come from the Caribbean and Latin America. At one end of the scale is light rum, typically from Cuba and Puerto Rico, and at the other are the dark rums of Jamaica, which are distilled and aged for longer. In between is a myriad of grades from all over the region and indeed the world. Light rum is the most mixable and is well-suited to cocktails, forming the basis of such classics as the Daiquiri and the Mojito.

TEQUILA

Distilled from the huge piñas of the blue agave plant, some form of tequila appears to have been around for hundreds and perhaps even thousands of years. It was originally enjoyed by the Aztec people of Mexico, and subsequently by the Spanish conquistadors who started to produce their take on it in the 16th century. It enjoys unprecedented popularity today, with a growing number of high-quality brands becoming widely available.

LIQUEURS, JUICES AND BITTERS

BUILDING BLOCKS WITH A MILLION COMBINATIONS

VERMOUTH AND APERITIFS

Vermouth has been a staple of the cocktail bar for 200 years, bringing its botanical flavours to classics like the Martini, Manhattan and Negroni.
The name of this fortified wine originates from the German word for wormwood – *Wermut* – as this has always been a key botanical used to aromatize the base wine, and was once believed to have medicinal value. French vermouth is white and usually dry, while Italian vermouth is red and usually sweet.

LIQUEURS

Bold fruit, nut and other natural flavours are commonly brought to a cocktail through sweet liqueurs such as Cointreau (orange), Gabriel Boudier's crème de cassis (blackcurrant) or Frangelico (hazelnut). It is important to use liqueurs with caution as it tends to be easier to oversweeten a drink than it is to oversour it. Oversweetening can also be hard to undo. Overall, orange liqueur – also known as triple sec or the slightly sweeter curaçao – is the liqueur used most often in this book.

BITTERS

Originally created as medicines for minor ailments, bitters are highly concentrated blends of alcohol, water and botanical extracts that have become indispensable to the modern bartender. The most famous bitters are those by Angostura, for which only five people know the closely guarded recipe. Other useful bitters to stock are orange bitters and Peychaud's bitters. Today, there are a growing number of bartenders infusing their own unique flavours.

A cocktail's complex flavour profile is built up by adding one or more of these ingredients to a base spirit. Citrus, bitters and alcohol can balance the sweetness that juices and liqueurs provide. Never be afraid to try varying ratios to match your personal taste.

FRUIT JUICE

Always squeeze your own citrus juice. You'll usually need the zest or a slice of it for garnish anyway, and bottled citrus juice is no replacement. Other juices can be impractical to squeeze yourself and are used less often, so buy multipacks of single-serving cartons of juices such as cranberry, pineapple and apple to ensure you always have a constant supply in the fridge.

SUGAR SYRUP

Most cocktails require added sweetness, usually in the form of sugar syrup (also called 'simple syrup'). Buy it in bottles or make your own by adding two parts sugar to one part hot (not boiling) water in a pan. Stir over a gentle heat, making sure not to boil or caramelize the sugar, until dissolved and pour into a bottle that has been rinsed with a shot of vodka. If you prefer to avoid refined sugar, you can use agave syrup in cocktails where its more amber colour and flavour are welcome. It tastes particularly good with tequila, as they are made from the same plant.

EGGS AND MILK

Some people are still uncomfortable with consuming uncooked eggs, though if they are from free-range, organic farms the risk of illness is highly remote. The mouthfeel and flavour that egg whites bring to a drink are unique, and powdered egg whites are available for those not comfortable with fresh. Milk and cream can equally make for a fine cocktail, from 'hard shakes' to the classic White Russian.

FINISHING TOUCHES
TURNING A MIXED DRINK INTO A FINE COCKTAIL

CITRUS

Use a vegetable peeler or small knife to take a wide strip of skin from the fruit, without including too much of the bitter pith. The oils from this are usually expressed into a drink to give extra flavour and aroma by folding it over the drink and wiping around the rim. Thin twists, which are more for decoration, are created with a channel knife. These can then be wrapped around a straw to set the helix shape before draping over the glass rim.

FLAMED ZEST

This technique adds a more complex flavour and aroma to the right drink, and a little fiery theatre to your cocktail preparation. Try it with a Cosmopolitan or an Old Fashioned. Skim a disc of skin from the fruit – usually an orange – and set aside while you light your match. Allow the phosphorus to burn off and the flame to settle down. Hold the flame above but not directly over the drink and express the oil from the zest through the flame and onto your drink.

SKEWERED FRUIT

Cherries, fruit slices and leaves can be combined in a million ways on a cocktail stick for extra dramatic effect when serving mixed drinks. They can be skewered like a kebab and rested between the sides of the glass, attached to a fruit wedge mounted on the rim, or even balanced on a floating hollow 'boat' made from a juiced lime skin or a halved passionfruit.

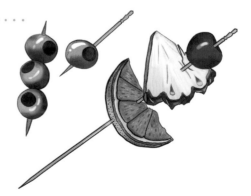

Just as we 'eat with our eyes', so we drink with them too. A cocktail's appeal is multiplied with artful presentation, and the key elements listed below are used throughout this book. Prepare your garnishes first so they will be ready as soon as your drink is mixed, ensuring optimal freshness.

ICE

You'll need ice for almost every cocktail, to both cool and dilute a drink as you shake or stir. It is best to either buy large bags made with mineral water from the supermarket, or freeze your own cubes with water from a filtering tap or jug.

An ice crusher is handy, though you can crush ice for drinks such as Mint Juleps and Zombies simply by wrapping cubes in a clean tea towel and bashing with your muddler.

RIM DUSTING

Dusting a rim with salt, sweet, or sour powder can add visual appeal and complementary flavours. To salt a Margarita rim, prepare your lime slice garnish and wipe round the rim to moisten it before tamping the glass upside down in a saucer of salt. This technique can be used for cocoa (with orange), cinnamon (with apple) and many other flavour combinations.

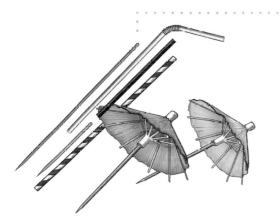

UMBRELLAS, STRAWS AND STICKS

Many drinks aficionados disapprove of the use of umbrellas, believing they undermine the seriousness of refined drinking. There are some cocktails, however, such as the Banana Daiquiri and the Singapore Sling, which somehow require a touch of flamboyant colour to complete the tropical theme. Keep a stock of standard cocktail sticks and straws (long and short), but don't be afraid to pick up novelty variants when you see them, as guests will love them.

GLASSWARE

SETTING THE STAGE FOR A SPECTACULAR SCENE

MARTINI

CHAMPAGNE
FLUTE

COLLINS

ROCKS

OLD
FASHIONED

BRANDY
(SNIFTER)

COUPE

TODDY

To make the cocktails in this book, and all well-known ones, you'll need the glasses shown here. You can however make the majority of cocktails if, to begin with, you have only the first four.

HIGHBALL

MARGARITA

HURRICANE

SLING

CHAMPAGNE SAUCER

CALIFORNIA COCKTAIL

JULEP CUP

COCKTAILS

7&7

Saturday Night Fever • 1977
Tony Manero / John Travolta

1½ oz / 37.5 ml blended whiskey
Lemon-limeade, such as 7UP or Sprite

Fill a Collins glass with ice, pour in the whiskey and top up with lemon-limeade. Stir lightly to mix without dispersing the fizz. Serve with a straw. This no-nonsense drink requires no fruit garnish.

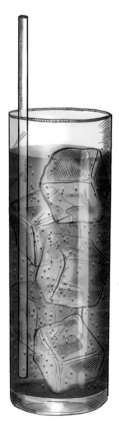

The 7&7 gets its name from the original recipe of Seagram's 7 Crown whiskey mixed with 7UP lemon-limeade. It was reportedly popularized by American soldiers in Vietnam and became one of the most commonly ordered drinks in the US in the 1970s. The two brands came together to create a series of advertisements with slogans such as 'America's Favorite Couple' well into the 1980s. Seagram's 7 has since declined in popularity and its availability is limited outside North America, so if you can't get it, try the recipe with your preferred Scotch whisky or with an Irish or North American blended whiskey instead for a fine, refreshing drink.

. . . .

Tony's the star of the famous light-up dancefloor at his local Brooklyn nightclub, 2001 Odyssey. In his little piece of 1970s New York, it's dancing prowess that makes him popular with the guys and sexy to the girls. While his friends settle racial and gang scores with their fists, Tony fights with his hips to be the king of the booming, disco-fuelled dance scene. And he only drinks one thing when he's there: a cool, crisp 7&7 to quench his thirst and keep him moving all night long.

AMBER MOON

Murder on the Orient Express • 1974
Beddoes / John Gielgud

1 raw egg
3 oz / 75 ml vodka
Tabasco sauce
Worcestershire sauce

Crack the egg into a Collins or Highball glass and pour in the vodka. Serve with Tabasco and Worcestershire sauce on the side to be added to taste, and a spoon for stirring. Whisky can be used instead of vodka, and the drink can be more palatable when blended.

This curious drink is really a variation on the Prairie Oyster, an old morning-after pick-me-up, with the addition of vodka to provide some hair of the dog. The practice of drinking a whole egg, or yolk, with added dashes of spicy sauce and vinegar is thought to be a quick fix for hangovers: the shot of nutrients and strong flavours serve to wake up the mind, body and most definitely the stomach.

. . . .

In Istanbul, Hercule Poirot boards the Orient Express to make his way back to England, the Belgian detective's adopted home. On the train he meets wealthy American businessman Samuel Ratchett, who pleads with the famous sleuth to help him investigate death threats he's been receiving, and offers him $15,000 for his assistance. The case doesn't really interest Poirot, as he'd rather relax after his business trip. But as head waiter Beddoes finds the next morning, it'll take more than his daily Amber Moon to get Ratchett moving on this particular day. There's a murderer on the train, and Poirot must find them.

APPLE MARTINI

The Break-Up • 2006
Brooke Meyers / Jennifer Aniston

2 oz / 50 ml vodka
1 oz / 25 ml apple schnapps
½ oz / 12.5 ml lemon juice
½ oz / 12.5 ml Cointreau

Shake all the ingredients with ice and pour into a chilled Martini glass. Drop a cocktail cherry in to garnish and serve.

The Appletini, as it is often called, is one of the most popular Martini variants and has featured in many films and TV shows over the last 20 years. It even became the official drink at Facebook's HQ after founder Mark Zuckerberg tasted the drink at the premiere of *The Social Network*, in which this cocktail also appears. Its true origin is unknown, and there are an endless number of differing recipes for it. Here we recommend a recipe similar to that of the International Bartenders' Association (IBA), with lemon juice added so the drink avoids being too sweet and heavy.

. . . .

Brooke wants to make her ex-boyfriend-cum-roommate jealous in the hope of motivating him to work on their broken relationship. Her friend Addie has set her up with Paul, a nice but decidedly nerdy character who takes her out to dinner. At the outset of the date he remembers the advice of Brooke's ex and orders two Apple Martinis to get things started, though Brooke knows that this drink can light even the wettest wick, prudently asking for water too.

AQUA VELVA

Zodiac • 2007
Robert Graysmith / Jake Gyllenhaal

¾ oz / 19 ml vodka
¾ oz / 19 ml gin
½ oz / 12.5 ml blue curaçao
Lemon-limeade, such as 7UP or Sprite

Shake the first three ingredients with ice and pour into a Hurricane glass filled with ice. Top up with the lemon-limeade. Garnish with a lemon slice and a cherry skewered together on a cocktail stick, along with a cocktail umbrella and straw.

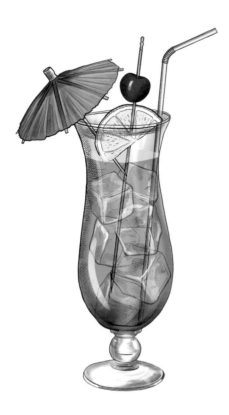

Aqua Velva was a popular, inexpensive aftershave during the 20th century. It was reportedly consumed by sailors during the Second World War due to its alcohol content and relative drinkability – as cheap grooming products go. It's not known when or where someone decided to create a cocktail in its name, but they concocted an appropriately lowbrow drink which, today, is mainly found atop sticky bars and sometimes garnished with a glowstick. Try replacing the spirits with tequila or rum and garnishing with mint for an interesting twist.

....

Robert, a newspaper cartoonist, is finally being taken seriously after he cracks the Zodiac killer's coded letter to the paper. When more cryptic messages arrive, crime reporter Paul asks him out for a drink. In a downtown bar Robert shamelessly orders the brightest, bluest drink – an Aqua Velva – complete with fruit garnish and paper umbrella. When serious drinker Paul can no longer contain his disdainful curiosity, Robert defends his choice: 'You wouldn't make fun of it if you tried it.' Sure enough, one exploratory slurp is all it takes to kick off a curaçao-tinged night of drunken deciphering.

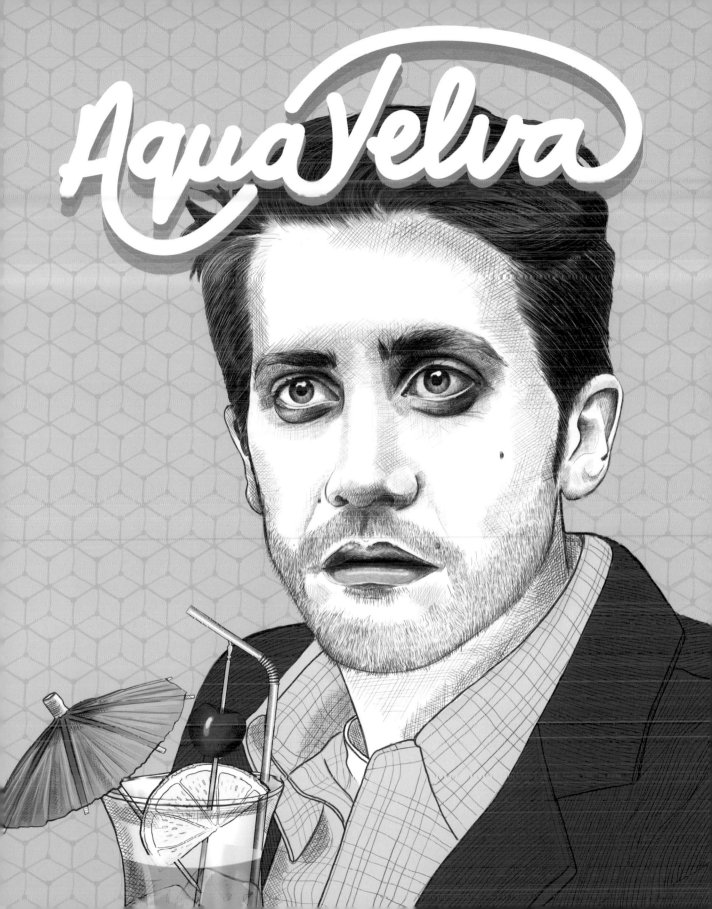

ARNOLD PALMER

The Other Guys • 2010
Allen Gamble / Will Ferrell

4 oz / 100 ml homemade iced tea
3 oz / 75 ml chilled water
1 oz / 25 ml fresh lemon juice
½ oz / 12.5 ml agave or sugar syrup
2 oz / 50 ml bourbon (optional)

Make the iced tea beforehand: pour boiling water into a jug, steep as many teabags in it as there are cups of water in the jug, add a teaspoon of sugar for each teabag, remove the teabags after five minutes and chill (preferably overnight).

Combine all the ingredients in an ice-filled Collins glass and garnish with a lemon slice. While this is a great mocktail to serve your guests, the addition of bourbon makes for a more grown-up Southern treat.

The story of almost every cocktail's inception has a generous splash of mystery and uncertainty in it, but not the Arnold Palmer. The man himself, one of the greatest professional golfers of all time, is still alive and can recount with clarity how he conceived and popularized the drink. He found it a refreshing post-game beverage and would order 'iced tea, with about a third of it lemonade'. Naturally, since he was a living legend in the golfing world, his bespoke drink was quickly copied in the clubhouses and restaurants he frequented and, before long, it became widely known by its creator's name. It is even available in cans bearing his face, with half a billion sold every year.

. . . .

Terry can't believe how stunning his partner Allen's wife is. She even makes him a hotel-grade breakfast every morning. Then they get a lead for their case: the guys who stole the pair's car and phone accidentally dialled Allen's ex-girlfriend. They pay her a visit to find out more, only to find yet another gorgeous and elegant woman. What's Allen's secret? We never quite know, but the ex's current beau is offensively dweebish, offering 'Arnie Palmies' to all while wearing chequered trousers.

BANANA DAIQUIRI

Up Close and Personal • 1996
Tally Atwater / Michelle Pfeiffer

2 oz / 50 ml white rum
1 oz / 25 ml fresh lime juice
½ oz / 12.5 ml banana liqueur
½ oz / 12.5 ml sugar syrup
½ a peeled banana

Place all the ingredients in a blender with a scoop or cup of crushed ice. Blend slowly at first, speeding up to create a light purée. Serve over ice in a Hurricane glass. To stay faithful to the movie, garnish with a cherry and pineapple wedge skewered on a long cocktail stick, but if you're feeling creative with your garnish, this is a drink that will accommodate even the most flamboyant dressing.

The Mountain Top Bar in St Thomas, US Virgin Islands, claims to be the 'home of the Banana Daiquiri', proudly serving it to this day in a popular stop-off point for tourists that take excursions to the mountain for its stunning views over the Caribbean coastline. It is claimed that in 1953 a British sea captain called George Soule searched the Caribbean for the region's finest cocktail. After sampling the best of several islands, he came upon a primitive version of the Banana Daiquiri in St Thomas, to which he added lime juice and a homemade banana liqueur. The Mountain Top's own recipe is still a secret.

Tally's the new girl on Philadelphia's Channel 7 News team, having moved from the sunnier climes of Miami. But she's not resonating well with the viewers or current female anchor Marcia, whose welcome is colder than Philly's icy winter winds. The pair go out for drinks with the station's bosses and Tally's characteristically Floridian drink choice of a Banana Daiquiri reminds Marcia of Spring Break in Fort Lauderdale, where we can only imagine what this highly drinkable libation was responsible for.

Banana Daiquiri

BAY BREEZE

Red Eye • 2005
Lisa Reisert / Rachel McAdams

2 oz / 50 ml vodka
3 oz / 75 ml cranberry juice
3 oz / 75 ml pineapple juice

Shake all the ingredients with ice and serve in an ice-filled Highball glass. Garnish with a lime slice.

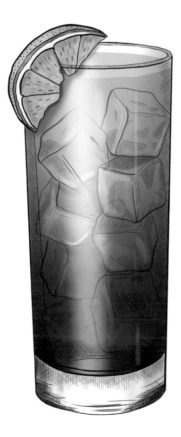

The Bay Breeze is a variation on the Sea Breeze, with pineapple juice taking the place of grapefruit juice for a sweeter, and – if shaken – frothier drink. There are many twists on the Breeze (or Cape Codder) family of drinks, which hinge on the combination of vodka and cranberry juice, which was reportedly popularized by the cranberry growers' cooperative Ocean Spray in the 1940s. The various Breeze drinks became popular in the 'dark ages' of cocktails, the 1960s, an era of oversweetened, colour-saturated drinks built using flavour powders, long-life juices and not an ounce of subtlety or sophistication. Thankfully the Bay Breeze made it out alive. Made with good-quality ingredients, it is a well-balanced drink for any occasion.

. . . .

Lisa just wants to get home but her Miami flight is delayed and tensions are running high at Dallas Airport. She bumps into a charming man called Jackson Rippner in the queue and ends up whiling away the delay at the airport bar with him. His knack for divining her favourite drink is almost spookily accurate: he guesses she's a Sea Breeze girl, but she insists her preference is a Bay Breeze, which she promptly orders. She doesn't seem to enjoy the drink too much, so maybe he guessed right. As they knock back their drinks, he jokes about being a murderer, but somehow his piercing blue eyes and mellifluous way with words drown out the alarm bells – until she's strapped into her seat and there's no escape.

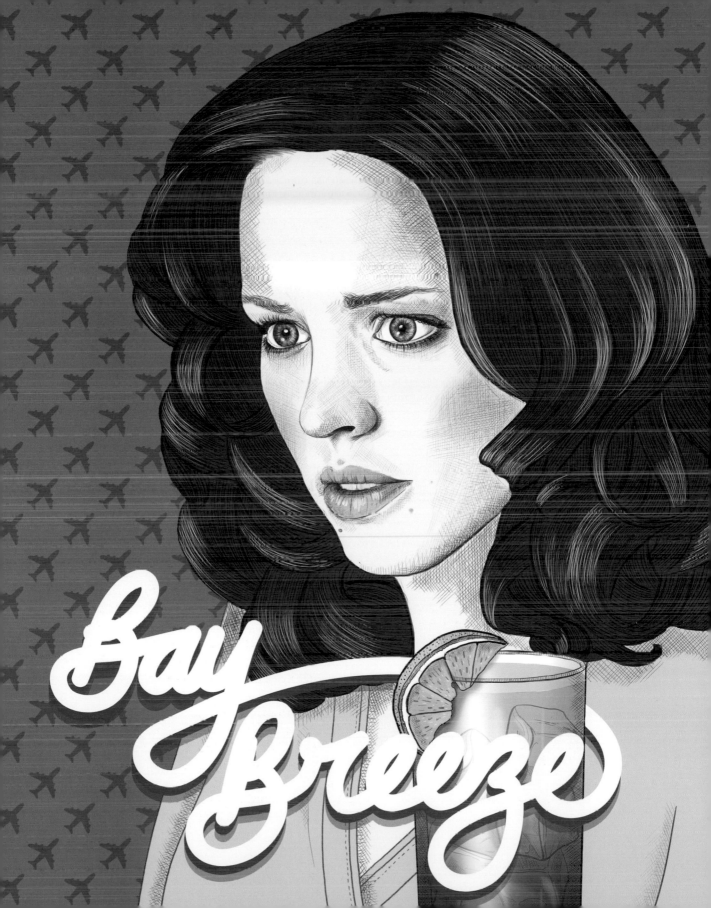

BLOODY MARY

Fletch • 1985
Fletch / Chevy Chase

1½ oz / 37.5 ml vodka
3 oz / 75 ml tomato juice
½ oz / 12.5 ml lemon juice
3 dashes Worcestershire sauce
6 drops Tabasco sauce
2 pinches ground black pepper
1 pinch celery salt

Gently shake all the ingredients with ice for at least half a minute before pouring into an ice-filled Highball glass. Serve with a celery stick.

The true origins of the Bloody Mary are disputed, but the combination of vodka and tomato juice became popular in the 1920s, reportedly because it was a regular bespoke order from comedian George Jessel at New York's famous 21 Club. Fernand Petiot, an illustrious bartender at Harry's New York Bar in Paris, claims to have taken that simple mix further to create what we know today as the Bloody Mary, with the addition of 'four large dashes of salt, two dashes of black pepper, two dashes of cayenne pepper, a layer of Worcestershire sauce and a dash of lemon juice'. He would serve the resulting cocktail in his bar, which was frequented by such luminaries as Ernest Hemingway, Humphrey Bogart and Coco Chanel.

· ·

Fletch needs to find out more about the deal he's just been offered by Alan Stanwick, a millionaire who is prepared to pay $50,000 for the pleasure of being murdered in his own home in order to avoid a slow, painful death from bone cancer and allow his family to cash in his life insurance policy. Fletch's investigations take him to the tennis club on a hot day, where he sneaks in, wearing the requisite whites, to get close to Stanwick's wife. When the waiter asks him for a membership card, he lies that he is with the Underhills, a haughty couple who deserve to have a Bloody Mary and two steak sandwiches put on their account.

BRANDY ALEXANDER

Two Lovers • 2008
Leonard Kraditor / Joaquin Phoenix

2 oz / 50 ml brandy
2 oz / 50 ml crème de cacao
2 oz / 50 ml single (light) cream

Shake all the ingredients with ice and strain into a chilled Martini glass or, as in this movie, a brandy 'snifter'.

A number of origin stories exist for this lush, creamy drink. Rumour has it that an original gin-based version of the cocktail was created in honour of Russian tsar Alexander II, though a bartender by the name of Troy Alexander at Rector's in New York is said to have concocted it for a themed event which required white drinks to be served. It appears in print as early as New York bartender Patrick Gavin Duffy's *The Official Mixer's Manual* of 1934, in which the gin and brandy variants are detailed as Alexander and Alexander No. 2 respectively. Duffy also provides a recipe for Alexander's Sister, which is made with crème de menthe instead of crème de cacao.

Leonard is a young photographer with lots of emotional baggage. Working at his parents' dry cleaning business every day isn't the glamorous life he might have dreamed of. Then he meets two beautiful women in quick succession. Michelle, the blonde unobtainable one, is sophisticated but also very much in love with Ronald, a successful senior lawyer. Leonard and the two women decide to go out for a friendly dinner. While the confused, depressed Leonard waits for them in a swanky New York restaurant he's pressed for his drink order. Suddenly he remembers Ronald's favourite drink – the Brandy Alexander – surely a shortcut to refinement, though not when nervously slurped through the garnish straw!

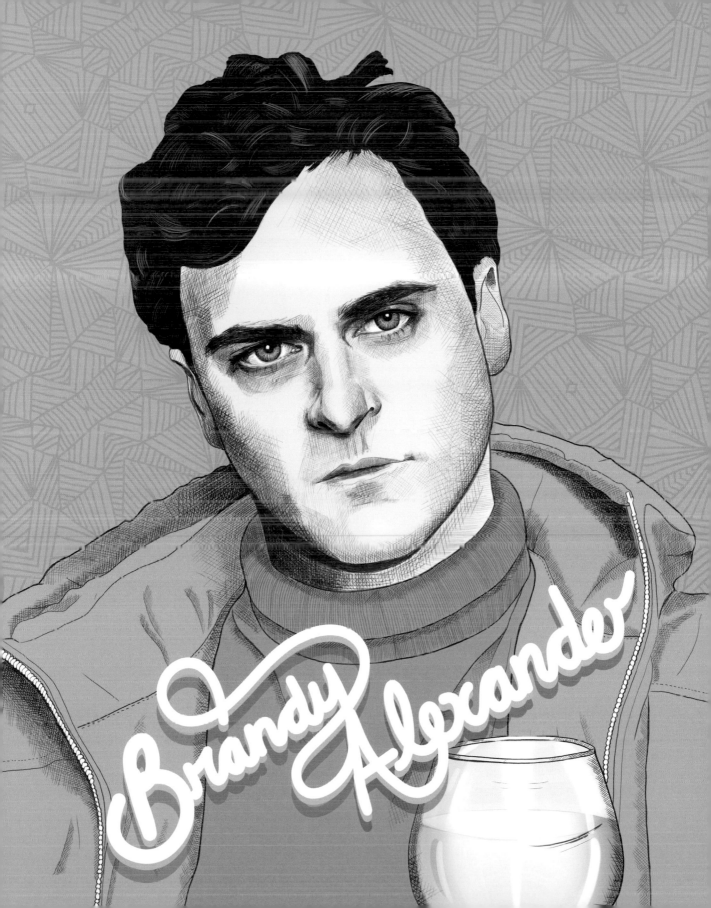

Brandy Alexander

BRONX

The Thin Man • 1934
Nick Charles / William Powell

1½ oz / 37.5 ml gin
¾ oz / 19 ml sweet vermouth
¾ oz / 19 ml dry vermouth
¼ of an orange

Pour the first three ingredients into your shaker. Squeeze the orange in, discarding the fruit once squeezed. Shake with ice and strain into a chilled coupe.

The Bronx is closely related to the Martini, and seems to have come into being in the early 20th century. It is the first known cocktail to contain fruit juice. The recipe used here is from Patrick Gavin Duffy's *The Official Mixer's Manual*, which was published in the same year *The Thin Man* was released. It is accompanied there by a Dry Bronx variation, which adds a slice of pineapple and requires muddling of the fruit. The classic version of the drink has remained largely unchanged, with today's IBA recipe differing only in that it contains very slightly less dry vermouth.

Two prominent origin stories exist, both from the dawn of the 20th century. Johnnie Solan at the bar of the Waldorf Astoria in New York reportedly met the challenge of creating it as a new cocktail to sell there, while Joseph S. Sormani apparently discovered the cocktail in Philadelphia and was later credited in his *New York Times* obituary as its originator. We'll never know either way, though their simultaneous timing suggests that one may well have discovered the other's invention rather than coming up with it himself.

· ·

Famous New York detective Nick Charles and his wife Nora are back in their hometown to catch up with friends. It's been a while since their move to San Francisco and it feels good to be back among acquaintances, in bars where all the waiters know them. Nick's a seasoned drinker, and quite the expert on mixology. As he explains to the attentive bartenders, the important thing about mixing drinks is the rhythm with which you shake: a Manhattan must be shaken to a foxtrot, a Dry Martini to waltz time and a Bronx to a two-step. Does it really matter? Try it for yourself, you'll see.

CHAMPAGNE CUP

The Grand Budapest Hotel • 2014
M. Gustave / Ralph Fiennes

1 oz / 25 ml brandy
½ oz / 12.5 ml orange liqueur
1 tsp Maraschino cherry syrup
Champagne

Stir the first three ingredients with ice and strain into a champagne saucer. Top up with champagne and drop a Maraschino cherry in the glass.

Champagne or claret 'cups' appear in the earliest cocktail books and were clearly popular, though the origin of the cup style of drink is unknown. In Jerry Thomas's *How to Mix Drinks* of 1862 the author describes the drink as excellent, and suggests it ought to be called the 'nectar of the Czar' due to its popularity in Russia 'amongst the aristocracy of the Muscovite empire'. His recipe is similar to the modern one, though with more vegetation, some sherry and what he describes as 'ratafia of raspberries' – an old term for fruit steeped with sugar in alcohol. Today's best equivalent would be the syrup of Maraschino cherries, or a liqueur such as Chambord.

....

After an epic journey conquering mountains, prisons, forests and vicious criminals, M. Gustave has finally proved his innocence, and can once again return to the Grand Budapest Hotel. He loves it dearly, and it loves him back. As he relaxes in the bar, sipping a Champagne Cup with the rich, blonde, older ladies of whom he is so fond, he can now reflect on his triumph against all odds. Zero will take over his concierge duties and in time inherit his mentor's fortune, but even in middle age his protégé can never leave this monumental relic of a bygone age.

COSMOPOLITAN

Sex and the City • 2008
Carrie Bradshaw / Sarah Jessica Parker

1½ oz / 37.5 ml vodka
1 oz / 25 ml triple sec
1 oz / 25 ml fresh lime juice
2 oz / 50 ml cranberry juice
1 dash orange bitters

Shake all the ingredients with ice and fine strain into a chilled Martini glass. Garnish with an orange twist, flamed if you dare.

The 'Cosmo' was probably born sometime in the late 1980s, though there are many who claim to have created and evolved this drink. It enjoys enduring popularity due to its accessibility to the infrequent cocktail drinker and having enough depth of flavour to keep even the most experienced palate interested, particularly with the addition of bitters and an orange twist. The drink's regular appearances in *Sex and the City* as the girls' favourite drink made it a staple of bars in the 1990s, cementing it as a modern-day classic.

. . . .

After the trials and tribulations of love lost, broken hearts, break-ups and reconciliations, the girls meet for Samantha's milestone 50th birthday. They're back in the trendy Meatpacking District at a bar full of hip New Yorkers. The girls sip their signature Cosmopolitans, pausing for a moment to savour that unique ensemble of flavours which now represents their younger days of fun and freedom, but also of uncertainty and insecurity. They're wiser and ultimately happier now. When Miranda asks the group why they ever stopped drinking their beloved Cosmos, Carrie sums it up beautifully: because everyone else started.

DAIQUIRI

Our Man in Havana • 1959
Jim Wormold / Alec Guinness

2½ oz / 62.5 ml light rum
¾ oz / 19 ml lime juice
½ oz / 12.5 ml sugar syrup

Shake all the ingredients with ice and strain into a chilled coupe. Float a lime wheel on the drink.

The Daiquiri is a cocktail with a definite birthplace, the town of Daiquirí in Cuba. American mining engineers working at the nearby iron mine at the end of the 19th century made the best use of local products – limes, sugar and rum – to create this popular classic. Early recipes in cocktail books show a dash of grenadine instead of (or with a lower proportion of) sugar syrup. There are now a number of widely known variations served in bars, from slightly different proportions (such as Embury's 8:2:1 and the 'countdown' 3:2:1) to the Hemingway Daiquiri, created for the author at La Floridita in Havana, with the addition of 1 oz / 25 ml Maraschino liqueur and ¾ oz / 19 ml grapefruit juice.

Jim's been in Havana for 15 years now. He feels like a local, though he's still very much an Englishman. His daughter Milly is coming of age and his vacuum cleaner shop isn't doing too well. Times might be getting tough but he enjoys Cuban bars, where he meets fellow expatriates for Daiquiris, sometimes shaken, sometimes frozen. While being served the crushed ice variant in a favourite watering hole, he's approached by a mysterious English gent with an unexpected proposition. Will Jim be our man in Havana?

DIRTY MARTINI

Iron Man 2 • 2010
Natalie Rushman (Natasha Romanoff) / Scarlett Johansson

2 oz / 50 ml gin
½ oz / 12.5 ml dry vermouth
¼ oz / 6 ml olive brine

Shake all the ingredients with ice and fine strain into a chilled Martini glass. Garnish with a thin lemon twist.

No-one knows who first spilled brine from the olive jar into their Martini and christened the mistake a Dirty Martini. There are rumours of Russian drinkers adding brine to their vodka as a hangover cure, and many attribute the cocktail to the unusual tastes of US President Franklin D. Roosevelt, who was known among his friends for creating challenging concoctions at his home bar. Indeed, if the Dirty Martini is made badly it can be the worst drink imaginable, particularly if you don't take care to ensure that the olive juice you use is in fact brine, and not oil or a flavoured mix of the two.

. . . .

Fresh from narrowly surviving an impromptu public rendezvous with Ivan Vanko in Monaco, Tony Stark could be having his last birthday. With the palladium spreading from the ARC reactor in his chest and making his blood toxic, he's starting to feel vulnerable. As he prepares for the party, his stunning new assistant shakes him a drink to start the night, a Martini served straight up and dirty. She seductively asks Tony if it's dirty enough for him, but mortality is heavy on his mind. How will he spend what he thinks might be his last birthday? Dancing in his Iron Man suit, of course!

DRY MARTINI

After Office Hours • 1935
Jim Branch / Clark Gable

2½ oz / 62.5 ml gin
½ oz / 12.5 ml dry vermouth

Stir the ingredients in a stirring or mixing glass with ice for about 30 seconds, then strain into a chilled Martini glass. To garnish, peel a strip of zest from a lemon, fold it lengthways over the drink to express the oils, wipe it around the rim, twist it and drop it into the drink.

When looking at the evolution of cocktails from the 19th century through to the present day, it becomes apparent that the Martini has become drier over the years. It appears in Harry Johnson's 1882 *Bartender's Manual* as being 1:1 gin and dry vermouth, while a more recent book, Duffy's 1934 *Official Mixer's Manual*, has it at 2:1. Later, David Embury's classic *The Fine Art of Mixing Drinks* from 1948 suggests 7:1, but states that the proportions can vary according to taste. The ratio can be as much as 10:1 for the driest of Martinis, at which point you can employ the vermouth rinse – rinsing the glass with vermouth before pouring back into the bottle – or use an atomiser to spray vermouth over the iced gin.

. . . .

Jim's an unstoppable newspaper editor with charisma and charm who is always after a story. While he's investigating a high-society love triangle, one of the trio is murdered. This story just got a whole lot juicier. Sharon, the society girl whom he just fired from her post as music critic, might just be his way into the upper echelons of society – and to the killer. As he courts her, taking her to elite hangouts and sipping Dry Martinis, Jim starts to realize he is slowly falling head over heels in love with this girl. Can he stay focused on the case?

DUBONNET COCKTAIL

Tootsie • 1982
Michael Dorsey (Dorothy Michaels) / Dustin Hoffman

2 oz / 50 ml Dubonnet Rouge
2 oz / 50 ml gin
1 dash orange bitters

Combine the first three ingredients in a shaker with ice. Shake and strain into a chilled Martini glass. Fold the lemon peel over the glass to express the citrus oils before twisting the peel and placing it in the drink.

Dubonnet is a fortified wine-based aperitif flavoured with herbs and spices. It was originally created in the 1830s by Joseph Dubonnet after the French government offered a reward to anyone who could find a way of promoting the consumption of quinine among the French Foreign Legionnaires in North Africa, due to the chemical's antimalarial properties. The Dubonnet Cocktail first appeared in literature in the early 20th century and was well known as the Queen Mother's tipple of choice, as it was for many others in the upper classes, who had acquired a taste for it while sojourning in the South of France. To this day it remains Queen Elizabeth II's favourite lunchtime drink – heavy on the gin, served in a rocks glass and with the lemon twist beneath the ice.

. . . .

Actor Michael Dorsey is frustrated and becoming increasingly unemployable. Taking a fresh approach – disguising himself from head to toe as a woman – has finally won him a part in a television soap opera: a dream job. But having attended the casting as Dorothy Michaels, he must keep up this persona and the double life that goes with it, so he urgently needs more dresses. He goes to the Russian Tea Room, where he knows George, his weary agent, will be having lunch, in the hope of borrowing money from him to go shopping. George doesn't even recognize him until he reveals himself vocally and orders a Dubonnet with a twist.

EGG NOG

The Awful Truth • 1937
Jerry Warriner / Cary Grant

3 oz / 75 ml milk
1 dash vanilla extract
⅓ stick of cinnamon
1 egg
1 oz / 25 ml sugar syrup
2 oz / 50 ml double (heavy) cream
2 oz / 50 ml dark rum or bourbon

Warm the milk and cream with the spices. Whisk the egg and sugar syrup together until thick, and then add the warm milk slowly as you whisk. Now pour into a saucepan and cook on a medium heat, avoiding boiling the mixture by stirring constantly. After 4 minutes, pour into a glass container and leave to cool. Add the alcohol and refrigerate, preferably overnight. Serve in a Collins glass with a dusting of nutmeg.

Today's Egg Nog is a Christmas staple in North America. Of late, the tradition has started to spread to distant shores, including the drink's ancestral home, England, where a drink called Posset, consisting of spiced hot milk curdled with ale or wine, was popular in medieval times. Over time this developed into Egg Nog with the addition of eggs and spirits. Its long American history stems back to the late 18th century and reveals the use of Caribbean rums and Southern bourbons at various times, based on availability. Either is recommended here and they can be relied upon equally to warm the heart.

Jerry's supposed to have been in Florida for the last two weeks, but he really just stayed in New York so he could do what he liked. The only thing is, he's returned home to find his wife has a new friend in the continentally suave voice coach Armand. Mutual suspicions are rising and the pair are heading for a divorce. From a large silver punchbowl, Jerry serves Egg Nog – a perennially reliable social glue even for the most awkward of occasions. All, including the unwelcome music teacher, lap it up with delight.

FLAMING RUM PUNCH

It's a Wonderful Life • 1946
Clarence the Angel / Henry Travers

½ **cup / 100 g** cloves
6 oranges
½ **bottle** aged rum
½ **bottle** cognac
½ **cup / 130 g** sugar
2 pinches cinnamon
2 pinches ground nutmeg
20 oz / 500 ml warm apple cider
16 oz / 400 ml hot water
12 oz / 300 ml orange juice
6 oz / 150 ml lemon juice

Stick the cloves in the oranges and bake in a medium oven for 30 minutes, until they soften. Place in a punchbowl and pour over the rum and cognac, followed by the sugar. Light the rum and, once alight, sprinkle over the spices. After around 20 seconds pour in the cider, water and juices slowly. As you do so, the flame will extinguish. Ladle into toddy glasses and garnish with a light sprinkle of ground nutmeg.

Punches are as ancient as the spirits with which we make them. First seen in the West in the early 17th century, it is thought that the drink was brought by early commercial sailors to Britain from India. The name is derived from the Sanskrit word for five (*panch*), indicating the original number of ingredients: spirits, water, lemon juice, sugar and spice. Initially, Western punches contained wine or brandy, but as Caribbean rum became available it grew into the most popular base spirit. Here we use equal parts of cognac and rum, partly to hark back to those early days of Punch served in dank taverns and heated by plunging a hot poker into the drink, but chiefly due to the sensationally fiery depth of flavour when the drink is served warm.

. . . .

George is starting to believe that his new friend Clarence might just be the guardian angel he claims to be, sent from heaven to save him from suicide. Having dried off from their plunge into the freezing river, they walk through the Bedford Falls that could have been, the one with no George Bailey, and dominated by the ruthless Mr Potter. In this alternate universe they enter Martini's bar to see it's a smoky, boozy den called Nick's. Clarence, being the 292-year-old angel he is, orders what he knows – a Flaming Rum Punch, or maybe a Mulled Wine. Either would be perfect to warm their frozen selves, but all his talk of wings and angels sees them being thrown face-first back into the bitter snow.

FRENCH 75

Casablanca • 1942
Rick Blaine / Humphrey Bogart

1½ oz / 37.5 ml gin
½ oz / 12.5 ml lemon juice
¼ oz / 6 ml sugar syrup
Champagne

Shake the first three ingredients with ice.
Pour into a champagne saucer and top
up slowly with champagne. Garnish with a
lemon twist.

The popular story of the provenance of the
French 75 is that British soldiers stationed
in France during the First World War put
together the key ingredients at their disposal
– London gin from home and the local
champagne – to create a punchy drink, which
they named after the iconic French M1897
75mm artillery gun. From the war-torn fields
of France, the drink was brought to America
and started to be served by the country's
pioneering bartenders during Prohibition
(America's dry period lasted from 1920 to
1933). The French 75 first appears in print in
Harry (of Harry's New York Bar in Paris fame)
MacElhone's book *Harry's ABC of Mixing
Cocktails* and quickly went on to become
a modern classic.

· ·

Everyone seems to find themselves at Rick's
Café Américain: soldiers, politicians, refugees,
gamblers, Nazis and exiled Americans like
Rick. As the Second World War rolls across
Europe, this corner of North Africa is a
refuge but also a prison for those who just
want to go home, though who knows what
home is like now. At Rick's bar you can
almost forget about the horrors of a world
in turmoil. The jazz plays sweetly and the
drinks flow freely, while drinkers of fine
wines, spirits and cocktails momentarily
put aside their differences to relax with Rick
who, when asked his nationality, claims to be
'a drunkard'. That, as Captain Renault says,
'makes Rick a citizen of the world'.

GIBSON

All About Eve • 1950
Margo Channing / Bette Davis

1⅔ oz / 42 ml gin
⅓ oz / 8 ml dry vermouth

Stir the ingredients in a stirring or mixing glass with ice, then strain into a chilled Martini glass. Garnish with a pearl onion on a cocktail stick and, optionally, a lemon twist.

The recipe offered here is from the 1954 *Esquire's Handbook for Hosts*, published only a few years after *All About Eve*'s release. The recipe has remained unchanged to this day, and is essentially a very dry Martini with the addition of a pearl onion.

No-one can say for sure where the Gibson originated, but it appears to have come about in the early 20th century. Some stories revolve around a teetotaler ordering a cocktail glass of water, either to remain more sober than his Martini-guzzling clients or simply to fit in. The cocktail onion was used as a garnish to mark the dry man's drink. A more likely story is that very dry Martinis were served with an onion to distinguish them from other Martinis, back in the day when Martinis were normally served very 'wet', with as much vermouth as gin. Over time, all Martinis came to be served drier, and eventually the only feature distinguishing the Gibson from a Dry Martini was the presence of the pearl onion.

. . . .

Eve is obsessed with Margo's every move, as if she wants to be her. Margo's suspicion of her new assistant grows as she begins to see how Eve is using her deceptively humble charm to cunningly rise to the top of the entertainment world, perhaps eventually to supersede her idol. At Bill's grand birthday party, Margo is full of morbid self-pity, feeling like the fading star in a constellation of bright, young suns. She consoles herself with a succession of Gibsons. In her own words, she's 'embalming her corpse', as she demands the pianist soothe her soul with the morose 'Liebestraum' for a fifth time.

GIMLET

The Snows of Kilimanjaro • 1952
Harry Street / Gregory Peck

1½ oz / 37.5 ml gin
½ oz / 12.5 ml lime cordial

Stir the ingredients in a stirring or mixing glass with ice, then strain into a chilled Martini glass.

This most simple of drinks came about in the 1920s and has since varied, some serving it with added soda and sugar. The original, however, was simply 1:1 gin and lime cordial. Over the decades, like many cocktails, it has become more gin-heavy and therefore drier. A Vodka Gimlet also became popular towards the end of the 20th century, though gin's recent resurgence has seen it reinstated as the true Gimlet base spirit. No-one knows where the drink's name came from, though the word 'gimlet' does also mean a small, hand-held drilling tool – apt for a drink that is sharp and piercing, with the dryness of the gin and the tartness of the lime hitting you straight between the eyes.

Harry Street may well be spending his last days here, on the hot and dusty plains of Tanzania, after a thorn wound became severely infected and threatened his life. Lying on his bed, nursed by his wife Helen, he has time to reflect on his life as a writer, a successful yet ultimately unfulfilled one. He recalls his time in Paris, where he met Cynthia Green. They drank Gimlets, courted and fell in love. Despite poverty they lived a Parisian life rich with colour, but ultimately his wanderlust would draw him to Africa, and away from the one true love of his life.

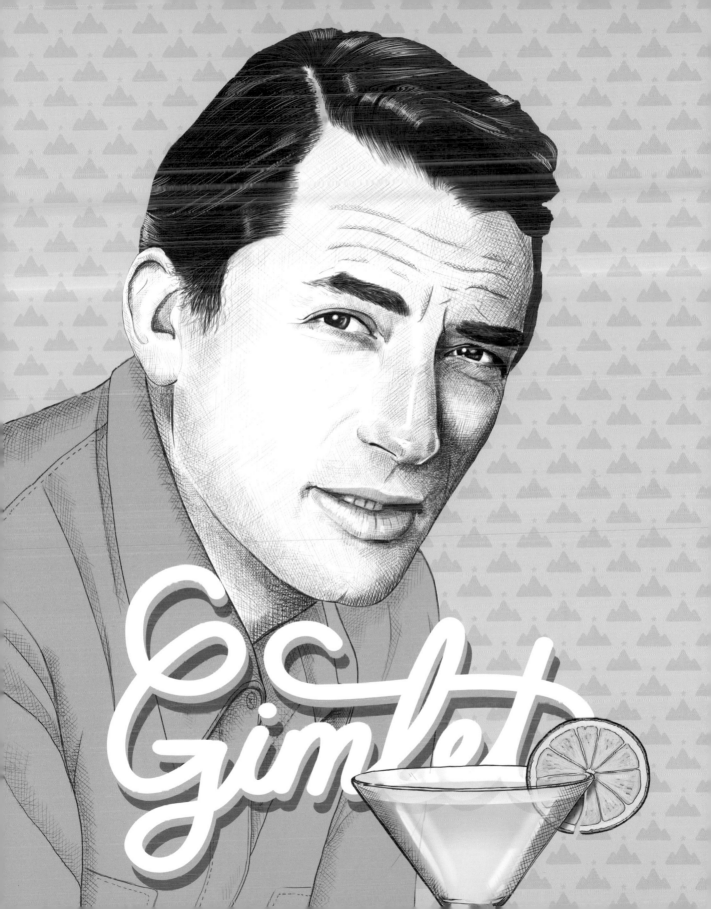

Gimlet

GRASSHOPPER

Romancing the Stone • 1984
Joan Wilder / Kathleen Turner

1 oz / 25 ml crème de menthe
1 oz / 25 ml crème de cacao
1 oz / 25 ml single (light) cream

Shake all the ingredients with ice and strain into a chilled California cocktail glass.

This after-dinner drink is alleged to have been created by the owner of Tujague's, a historic restaurant in the French Quarter of New Orleans. Philip Guichet created the recipe for a bartending competition in New York and won second place. He promptly started to serve the drink upon his return and it seems to have been on the establishment's menu since around 1919. It subsequently became popular in the Southern states of America and morphed into both a milkshake and an alcoholic dessert, in which varying amounts of ice cream take the place of the cream and the drink is whipped or blended.

Joan is a writer of romance novels, but she can never conjure up any love in her own life. Living alone with her cat, she doesn't seem to be able to meet the right men. All the guys in New York City seem so sleazy, egotistical or just weird. As she sits with her editor in a bar, surveying the talent and drinking Grasshoppers, she is unaware that far away in Colombia her sister has been kidnapped. Only Joan holds the key to her ransom and release.

GREEN CRÈME DE MENTHE FRAPPÉ

Funny Girl • 1968
Fanny Brice / Barbra Streisand

2 oz / 50 ml green crème de menthe
Shaved or heavily crushed ice

Fill a flute or California cocktail glass with shaved ice (you can make shaved ice either by freezing a block and shaving it with a grater, or smashing ice cubes in a tea towel until they are reduced to ice dust and small pieces). Drizzle the crème de menthe over the ice and serve with a short straw.

Crème de menthe is, as the name suggests, a French mint liqueur. It is usually made with Corsican mint, which is steeped in grain alcohol for several weeks before it is filtered and sweetened to create the final product. The liqueur is less popular nowadays, being associated with quaint, elderly drinking tastes and the dusty recesses of suburban liqueur cabinets, though it plays a vital role in classic cocktails such as the Grasshopper and Stinger. This preparation resembles a minty, boozy snow cone, and can equally be recommended with ice cream, either as an affogato or whipped up to make a thick shake.

· ·

As Fanny prepares to board the train to Chicago, a bunch of beautiful roses and a note from her lover Nicky arrives. She's not prepared to leave this relationship to chance for one more second, and jumps on the train to New York, where she must board a tugboat to catch Nicky's ocean liner. He's shocked and overjoyed to see her, and they make their way to the ornate dining room to talk about the future. In typical style he orders her a sophisticated European drink – a Crème de Menthe Frappé – before agreeing that they should indeed be married.

HIGHBALL

The Great Gatsby • 2013
Jay Gatsby / Leonardo DiCaprio

2 oz / 50 ml Scotch whisky
Soda water

Fill a Highball glass with ice, pour in the whisky and fill the glass up with soda. Take three cocktail sticks and skewer two cherries and a lemon slice on one, then skewer two cherries on each of the remaining sticks. Cut the end off a lemon to create a flat dome about the width of a golf ball and stand your two cherry sticks in the lemon end, which then sits atop the drink. Add the lemon and cherry skewer, a sprig of mint and a large, old-fashioned paper straw and your Gatsby Highball is complete.

Patrick Gavin Duffy claimed in his 1934 book *The Official Mixer's Manual* to be the man who had brought the Highball to America in 1894. He said he made them in response to British actors asking for Scotch and Sodas at his Midtown bar, though, like most cocktail inventions, this is not without contest from a number of mixologists around this time. While the Highball has come to mean the family of drinks in which a double spirit is served with a carbonated drink in a tall glass with ice – for example, a Gin and Tonic, or Rum and Cola – in the early 20th century Scotch and Soda was the most popular combination. The name is said to originate from the drivers of steam locomotives giving a 'highball' signal of two short whistle blows and one long, like the drink's recipe, to tell the conductor that the water tank was full – indicated by a ball float in the high position.

. . . .

Gatsby has turned up on Nick's doorstep with the beautiful machine that is the yellow Deusenberg. They take a dreamy ride into New York City to an unassuming barbershop. What lies beyond the steam and overpowering smell of shaving lotions is a clandestine Aladdin's cave of decadence, cabaret, the high-class people of New York and any cocktail you can imagine. The bar staff already know what Gatsby will want this lunchtime. 'Highballs', he echoes back to the waiter, and the table is filled with sumptuously garnished cocktails. Nick's not sure what he's getting into here, but he thinks he might just like it.

HORSE'S NECK

Caught in a Cabaret • 1914
Mabel / Mabel Normand

2 oz / 50 ml brandy
2 dashes Angostura bitters
Ginger ale

Pour the first two ingredients into an ice-filled Collins glass and top up with ginger ale. Garnish with a spiral of lemon zest.

The Horse's Neck started life in the late 19th century as a refreshing non-alcoholic drink. It was simply ginger ale on ice with a dash of bitters and lemon zest, and remains a great cooler to serve with summer lunches and picnics. In the early 20th century it started to be served with bourbon or brandy to give this horse a 'kick' – though brandy has become the dominant base spirit, appearing in the IBA's official recipe. By the 1960s it had become particularly popular with the Royal Navy, and was served regularly at naval cocktail parties. Perhaps sailors' (arguably unfair) reputation for hard drinking led Ian Fleming, in the 1966 James Bond novel *Octopussy*, to state that the Horse's Neck was the 'drunkard's drink'.

. . . .

It's such a scorching hot day that Charlie's dachshund – who is, as he says, 'built too near to the hot sidewalk' – needs cooling off. An inevitable caper ensues as Charlie tries to hydrate the hound in a fresh spring by the road. He falls into shrubbery, loses the dog and causes uproar when he pushes over the boy returning his furry friend. All the while society girl Mabel is preparing for her 'coming-out party', and in the hot midday sun she sensibly asks for a Horse's Neck to be mixed for her before embarking on an afternoon stroll. As she enters the woods with her beau, it's a stick-up! But an unlikely hero appears in the form of bumbling Charlie, who bravely saves Mabel and earns himself a 'tête-à-tête' at the young debutante's chic chateau.

LONG ISLAND ICED TEA

Cruel Intentions • 1999
Cecile Caldwell / Selma Blair

½ oz / 12.5 ml tequila
½ oz / 12.5 ml gin
½ oz / 12.5 ml vodka
½ oz / 12.5 ml light rum
½ oz / 12.5 ml triple sec
½ oz / 12.5 ml lemon juice
½ oz / 12.5 ml lime juice
¾ oz / 19 ml sugar syrup
Cola

Pour all the ingredients except the cola into an ice-filled Highball glass and top up with cola. Garnish with a lemon slice.

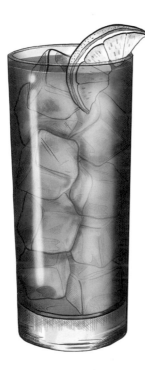

There are conflicting stories describing the birth of this boozy beverage. A bartender from New York who worked at the Oak Beach Inn on Long Island claims to have created the recipe in 1972, during a cocktail competition which required the use of triple sec. While there are numerous sources to support his claim, there are alternative origin stories going back as far as Prohibition, when the cocktail may have been one of many 'disguise drinks' that were created to look like iced tea while in fact being full of alcohol.

....

Kathryn is manipulating everyone, including the innocent Cecile and womanizing Sebastian, whom she's thrown together in a shrewd attempt to corrupt Cecile in revenge for losing her boyfriend to the naive virgin. At Sebastian's house, the willing corrupter gives Cecile iced tea, which she drinks with childlike gusto through a huge curly straw. As its inebriating effects start to take hold, Cecile questions whether this really is 'iced tea', and finds out too late that it's the kind from Long Island – the kind that can get you into big trouble, fast.

MAI TAI

Blue Hawaii • 1961
Chad Gates / Elvis Presley

2 oz / 50 ml aged rum
1 oz / 25 ml lime juice
½ oz / 12.5 ml curaçao
½ oz / 12.5 ml orgeat almond syrup
¼ oz / 6 ml agave syrup

Shake all the ingredients together and pour into an ice-filled rocks glass. Garnish with a pineapple wedge and cherry skewered together on a cocktail stick and mounted on the rim of the glass.

The godfather of tiki drinks, Trader Vic (born Victor Jules Bergeron), created the Mai Tai in 1944. It is one of many drinks he invented from his tiki-themed bar and restaurant in Oakland, California, which he founded in 1934. The company started to open franchises in 1940 and, riding the tiki culture boom of the 1950s and '60s, opened bars all over the world. Vic's 1947 book (and particularly the 1972 reprint) *The Bartender's Guide* is still considered one of the seminal books of mixology. Legend has it that when Vic asked some visiting friends from Tahiti to try a new drink he'd made, one of them exclaimed 'Maita'i roa ae!' which means 'very good!' in Tahitian. That original version of the Mai Tai is the one which appears here, though it has been modified countless times over the years, with the addition of orange, grapefruit and pineapple juices to make it sweeter and longer.

. . . .

Chad is home from the Army and his mother is so proud, though she can't accept he hasn't actually been in a war, and hates it when he puts his civvies back on. She is also seemingly addicted to Mai Tais, particularly with extra rum, and sips them almost constantly. Dad wants his son to experience their favourite tipple to celebrate his homecoming but Sarah Lee doesn't want her fine young boy to have 'intoxicating libations' just yet. She doesn't see why he must be a tour guide and musician, both of which seem to attract female fans, but when he hatches a plan for a travel business and declares his proposal to beautiful Maile, there's only one way for his proud parents to celebrate – a round of Mai Tais in Kaua'i, of course.

MANHATTAN

Some Like It Hot • 1959
Sugar Kane Kowalczyk
/ Marilyn Monroe

2 oz / 50 ml bourbon or rye whiskey
1 oz / 25 ml sweet vermouth
2 dashes Angostura bitters

Stir the ingredients in a stirring or mixing glass with ice for about 30 seconds, then strain into a chilled Martini glass. Garnish with a Maraschino cherry with a stalk (or skewer it).

Traditionally made with rye whiskey, the Manhattan is often served with bourbon today. Either works well in its own way and rye has enjoyed a resurgence in recent years. There are three key variations on the mix, and you will likely be asked for your preference when ordering a Manhattan at a reputable bar: dry, perfect and sweet. Dry Manhattans are made with dry vermouth, Perfect Manhattans with half dry, half sweet vermouth and a Sweet Manhattan is the recipe used here due to its popularity and palatability. For extra sweetness you can add a spoon of syrup from the jar of Maraschino cherries.

Though its true origins are unknown, the Manhattan became fashionable in the 1880s and went on to be a truly essential cocktail, variations on which could make up an entire mixologist's menu.

. . . .

Joe and Jerry are trying desperately not to attract attention. They've landed a gig in an all-girl band and are playing their female roles successfully so far. On the overnight train, Jerry's bunked up with a livewire in blonde bombshell Sugar Kane, and before long she's found half a bottle of bourbon. Before they can enjoy a quiet drink in their bunk together, another band member, Dolores, finds them. Sugar Kane suggests Manhattans and sends her off to get vermouth and the 'cocktail shaker' – a hot water bottle. Before long the whole giddy troupe is downing the sweet version of this enduring classic, but can Joe and Jerry make it through the night without blowing their cover?

MARGARITA

Boogie Nights • 1997
Eddie Adams (Dirk Diggler) / Mark Wahlberg

2 oz / 50 ml tequila blanco
½ oz / 12.5 ml triple sec
1 oz / 25 ml lime juice
1 teaspoon agave nectar

Combine all the ingredients in a blender with crushed ice and blend. For the classic non-frozen straight-up serve, shake and strain into either a chilled, salt-rimmed Margarita glass or an ice-filled rocks glass for a longer-lasting drink. Garnish with a lime wedge.

While the true origin of the Margarita is unknown, the drink initially became popular in the 1940s in Mexico and America, spreading further afield in the 1950s when it first started to appear in bartending books. It may be derived from a Daiquiri, or the 19th-century Daisy. The Margarita has been modified and mutated into a million colours, flavours and serving styles over the decades but the original version described here endures as the most ordered cocktail in many nations, including America. The three standard serving styles – straight up, frozen and on the rocks – are all delicious and highly recommended.

. . . .

Eddie Adams, the boy from Torrance, is welcomed into the arms of the adult film industry's elite, having turned his back on a broken home and the mother who threw him out. With his youthful looks and plenty of libido to spare, he's ready to be something good, even if that means being a good porn star. His first foray into this new world and the strange people who inhabit it is at film director Jack Horner's pool party. He meets a kindred spirit in fellow actor Reed Rothchild, who makes him a cool, salted Margarita, and with that his life as Dirk Diggler begins.

MARTINI

Batman • 1989
The Joker / Jack Nicholson

3 oz / 75 ml gin
1½ oz / 37.5 ml dry vermouth

Stir the ingredients in a stirring or mixing glass with ice for about 30 seconds, then strain into a chilled Martini glass. Garnish with an olive on a cocktail stick.

Experts are unsure as to the true origin of the Martini. Adding flavoursome ingredients such as bitters, vermouth and fortified wines to gin became popular in the late 19th century and vermouth manufacturers Martini & Rosso marketed their products as the perfect accompaniment to gin as early as 1863. It's not known if that brand was the originator of the cocktail's name, but its growing synonymy with the mix undoubtedly made it an easy shorthand for ordering gin stirred with vermouth. This recipe makes a relatively 'wet' Martini with the 2:1 ratio of gin to vermouth, and as seen in the movie, the colour will be slightly more amber.

· ·

Jack Napier hasn't been the same since his botched raid on Axis Chemicals ended with him being cornered by Batman and plunged into a noxious vat of chemical waste. Not only is he bizarrely disfigured, but he's taken on a maniacal flamboyance. Strangely, he's much happier now and can't wait to tell his beautiful mistress Alicia about his somewhat unorthodox makeover. As he sits waiting for her, sipping a Martini, she returns from a shopping spree only to collapse to the floor along with her bags of new clothes, stunned by his grotesque new countenance.

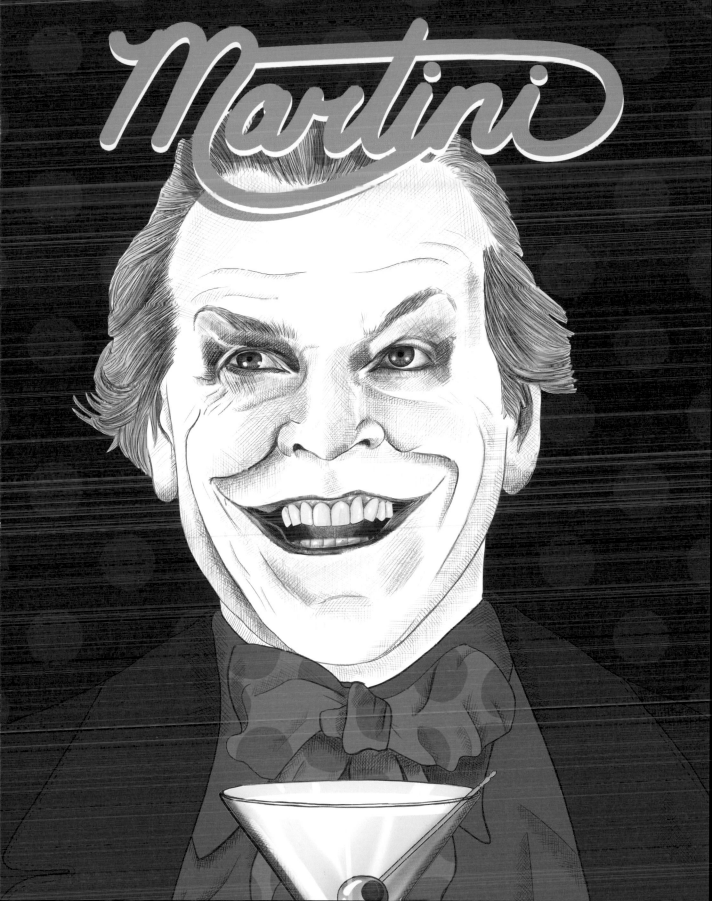

MIDNIGHT MARGARITA

Practical Magic • 1998
Sally Owens / Sandra Bullock

2 oz / 50 ml tequila añejo
½ oz / 12.5 ml triple sec
1 oz / 25 ml lime juice
½ oz / 12.5 ml raspberry liqueur

Squeeze your lime and use the discarded peel to wipe the rim of a rocks or Old-Fashioned glass. Place the glass upside down on a saucer of salt. Fill the glass with crushed ice. Shake the tequila, triple sec and lime juice with ice and strain it into your glass. Top up with crushed ice and drizzle the raspberry liqueur over it.

The Midnight Margarita is one of countless variations on this cornerstone cocktail. It serves as a sweet, accessible introduction to a whole category of drinks that it is hard not to love. In *Practical Magic*, the witches use a number of unconventional ingredients such as 'tongue of dog' and 'blindworm's sting', which we can't verify the effectiveness of here. Needless to say, they are not recommended. Instead we've added a drizzle of raspberry liqueur, which brings a dramatic, cauldron-like appearance to the drink, with streaks of purple through the crushed ice and a salty rim evoking the spume and sparkle of magic spells.

· ·

Sally and Gillian are no ordinary sisters. Raised by their aunts, they've been taught the ways of the witch. Life has its ups and downs when you're a practitioner of magic, and relationships certainly aren't easy. But there's one ritual that's a definite high – Midnight Margaritas! As the clock strikes twelve the girls and their aunts dance with joy around the blender, concocting a party potion. They pour in tequila, limes, sugar and the wool of bats (among other abominable ingredients), and finish it off with a magic spell to make the whole concoction a perfect witch's brew.

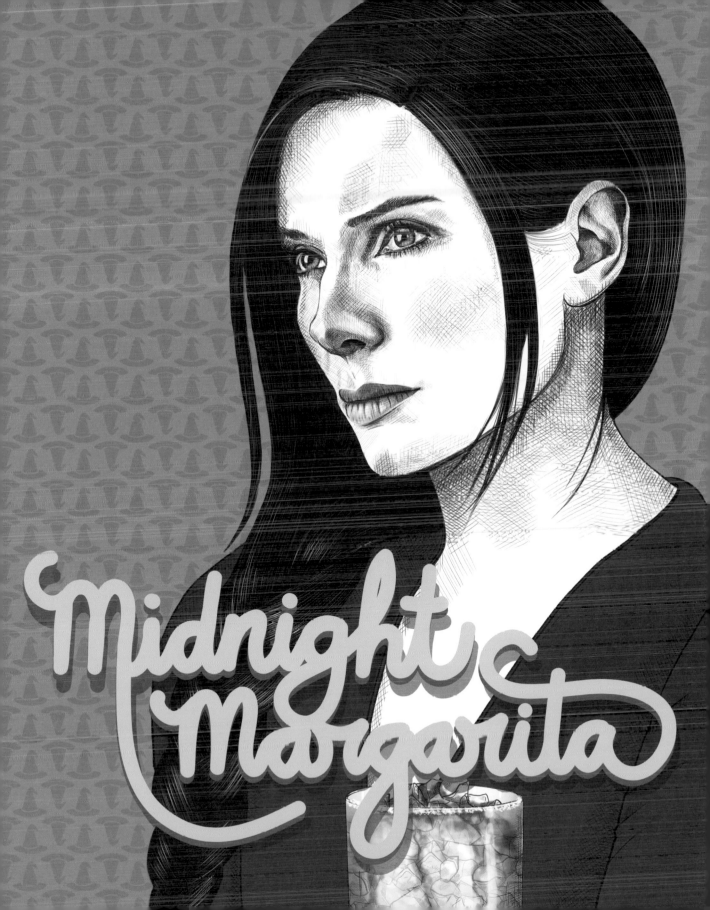

Midnight Margarita

MIMOSA

Rat Race • 2001
Vera Baker / Whoopi Goldberg

½ oz / 12.5 ml orange liqueur
2 oz / 50 ml orange juice
2 oz / 50 ml brut champagne

Pour the orange juice and liqueur into a champagne flute, then add the champagne. Garnish with a thin orange twist draped over the rim of the glass.

The Mimosa dates back to the mid-1920s, when it was reportedly created at the Ritz in Paris by Frank Meier, who was bartender there for 26 years and author of the 1934 book *The Artistry of Mixing Drinks*. In London around the same time, and perhaps even earlier, the Buck's Fizz was born at Buck's Club in Mayfair. This is essentially the same drink but with a 1:2 ratio of champagne to orange juice. There is some disagreement amongst mixologists on the merits of including triple sec or orange liqueurs such as Grand Marnier or Cointreau, but the added depth of flavour makes for a more interesting drink.

Vera hasn't seen her daughter in 27 years. Her psychic Lucianne says she should go looking for her, so she hires a private detective to find the baby she gave up all those years ago. As Vera waits in a Vegas hotel lobby, long-lost daughter Merrill arrives uptight and full of stress. After calming down and taking a deep breath, she starts to relax and open up. The reunited ladies are asked what they want to drink and simultaneously tell the waitress 'Mimosa'. And so their innate mother-daughter connection once again lights up, just in time for an epic adventure to unfold before them.

MINT JULEP

Thank You For Smoking • 2005
The Captain / Robert Duvall

10 mint leaves
½ oz / 12.5 ml sugar syrup
½ oz / 12.5 ml chilled water
2 oz / 50 ml bourbon

Half-fill a Julep cup or Collins glass with crushed ice. Add the mint, sugar and water and gently stir. Add the bourbon, fill the cup with crushed ice and stir until the outside is frosted. Garnish with a sprig of mint.

The Mint Julep is one of the most ancient cocktails, and as such its history is deep and murky. The earliest recorded mention appears to be in a tome from 1784 by the Society for Promoting Medical Knowledge, where it is suggested as a remedy for 'sickness of the stomach'. The drink goes on to make regular appearances in cocktail books throughout the 19th century, with brandy, gin and whisky used as frequently as bourbon. As the century progressed, the drink became more strongly associated with the Southern states of America and with the region's spirit – bourbon. In the 1930s the drink became the official cocktail of the Kentucky Derby, and in 2008 the host racecourse created the biggest ever Mint Julep. It measured 2.3 m (6 ft 7 in.) tall, including the mammoth mint sprig.

Nick has made quite a splash defending the tobacco industry in front of millions on *The Joan Show*. He's been summoned to see The Captain, a living legend of the industry and the man who first introduced filters when cigarettes started to be criticized in the press. As Nick descends into the members' club, he finds an old Southern gentleman enjoying an old Southern drink. The Captain explains that, to make a really good Mint Julep, you crush the mint against the ice with your thumb – while thumbing a sprig against his palm with quiet menace to demonstrate – to release the menthol. And the man who taught him that? Fidel Castro.

MISSISSIPPI PUNCH

Breakfast at Tiffany's • 1961
Holly Golightly / Audrey Hepburn

2 oz / 50 ml cognac
1 oz / 25 ml bourbon
½ oz / 12.5 ml lemon juice
½ oz / 12.5 ml sugar syrup
1 oz / 25 ml dark rum

Shake all the ingredients except the rum with crushed ice and pour into a Collins glass, unstrained. Top the glass with more crushed ice, gently pour over the rum and garnish with an orange slice and a cherry.

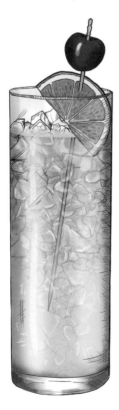

This highly alcoholic party drink appears in the earliest mixology book, Jerry Thomas's 1862 *How to Mix Drinks*, with this single-serving version. However, it can also be made in a punchbowl to the same proportions, with fruit such as oranges and berries added for a more 'punchy' taste and appearance. Some modern recipes leave out the rum, and if you do that and replace the cognac with pineapple juice, you have a Florida Punch.

....

The party is in full swing and the booze is flowing like a mountain river. Holly Golightly has thrown another of her infamous soirées, attracting friends and acquaintances from New York's wealthy socialite scene. As the cat with no name watches with bemusement from atop the furniture, the gathering descends into drunken debauchery, much to the chagrin of Mr Yunioshi upstairs. Just as he considers calling the police, more bourbon arrives, meaning more Mississippi Punch!

Mississippi Punch

MOJITO

Die Another Day • 2002
James Bond / Pierce Brosnan

10 mint leaves
1 oz / 25 ml lime juice
½ oz / 12.5 ml agave syrup
2 oz / 50 ml light rum
Soda water

Lightly muddle the mint leaves with the lime juice and agave syrup in a Collins glass. Half-fill the glass with ice, add the rum and stir. Fill the glass up fully with ice and top up with soda. Stir gently. Garnish with a lime wedge and a mint sprig.

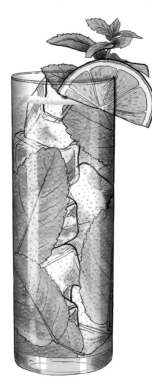

The Mojito was probably born in Havana, Cuba. It came to Europe via English sailors fighting in Central America during the Anglo–Spanish War in the late 16th century. Legend has it that Sir Francis Drake's ships suffered various food- and waterborne illnesses while raiding in the region, and as they neared Cuba a boarding party went ashore to find remedies. There they discovered a popular local remedy – a primitive form of rum mixed with lime, sugarcane and mint – used to cure various ills. Drake's men took it and found it effective for many complaints, including scurvy and dysentery. The drink became known as 'El Draque'. It is not known when this became today's Mojito or where the modern name comes from. However, a bar in old Havana, La Bodeguita del Medio, claims to be both where the drink was born in 1942, and where it became the favourite drink of many luminaries, including Ernest Hemingway.

. . . .

As Bond waits in the beach bar, avoiding the Cuban sun's merciless heat, he sips an ice-cold Mojito accompanied by a fine cigar – two of the Caribbean island's finest exports. He's posing as an ornithologist, and through his binoculars he has spied quite a bird on the water – agent Jinx Johnson. James offers her some of his Mojito as she dries off. The cocktail's a little strong for her palate, though she says she could get used to it in time. Fortunately they have all night.

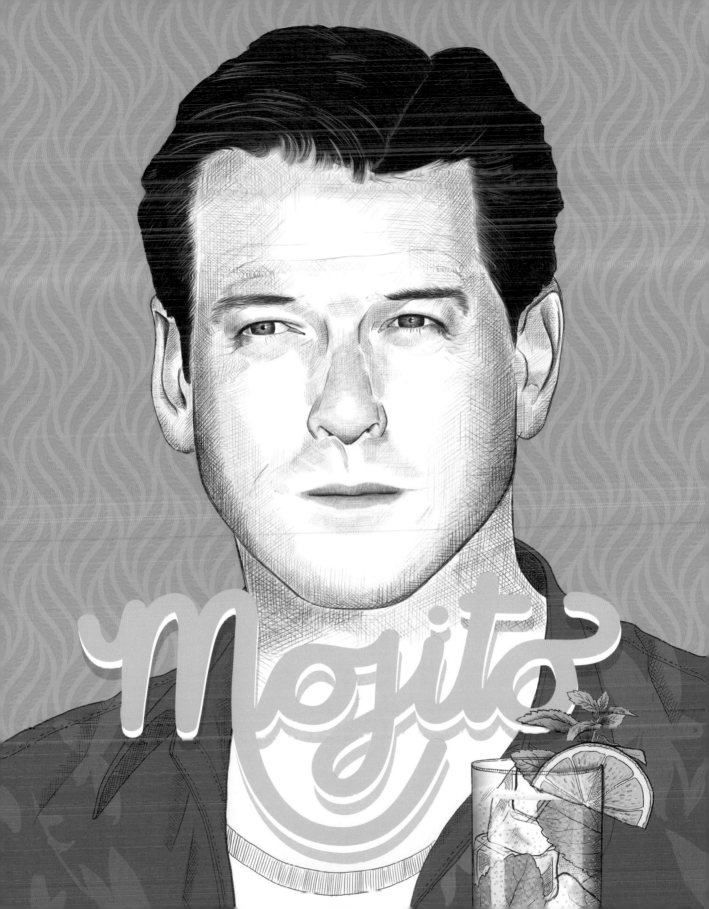

MOLOKO PLUS

A Clockwork Orange • 1971
Alex DeLarge / Malcolm McDowell

1 oz / 25 ml absinthe
1 oz / 25 ml anisette liqueur
2 oz / 50 ml Irish cream liqueur
5 oz / 125 ml milk
½ oz / 12.5 ml sugar syrup

Shake all the ingredients with ice and
serve in a Collins glass.

A completely fictional family of drinks,
Moloko Plus features in both Anthony
Burgess's original book and Stanley
Kubrick's film. In the book the various
versions of the drink have drugs added,
with 'vellocet' containing opiates,
'synthemesc' synthetic mescaline,
'dencrom' adrenochrome and more.
Many recipes exist for this fictitious drink.
The one here is the most popular and
contains absinthe to reflect the fictional
cocktail's psychoactive properties.

. . . .

Alex DeLarge and his grotesque gang,
or 'droogs' as he calls them in his native
Nadsat dialect, are getting high on Moloko
Plus in the stark Korova Milk Bar. With the
arrogance of youth they lounge on statues
of naked women, sipping Moloko Plus of
various varieties – uppers, downers, mind-
twisters. Looking blankly into the distance
as they sip the long, white drinks, they
prepare for their favourite pastime of all –
a 'bit of the old ultraviolence'.

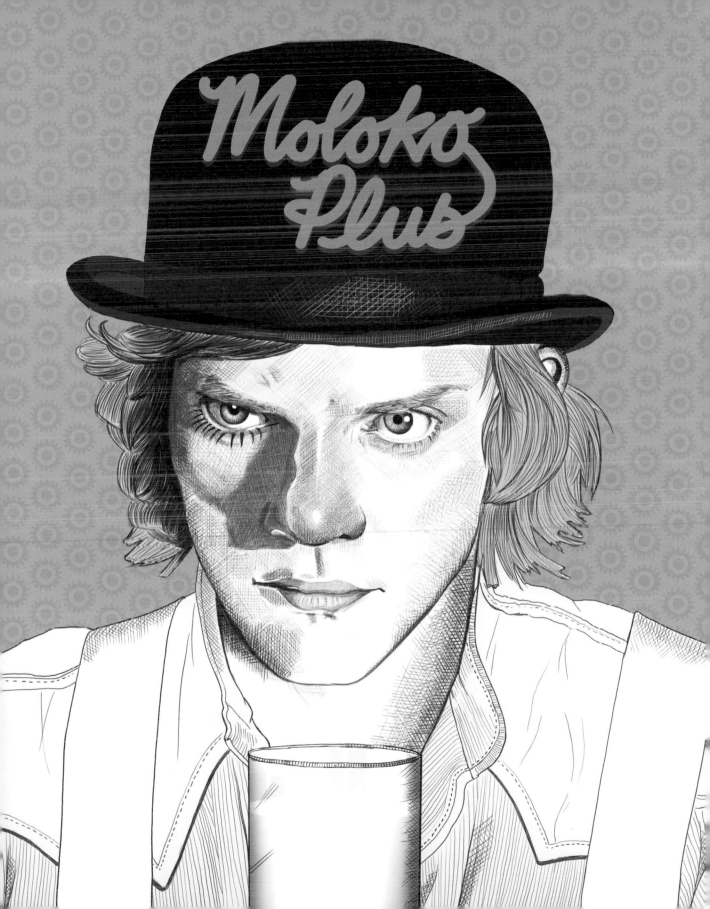

MULLED WINE

Amélie • 2001
Amélie Poulain / Audrey Tautou

26.4 oz (750 ml) bottle of red wine
2 oz / 50 ml sloe gin
2 sticks cinnamon
12 cloves
1 pinch ground nutmeg
1 large piece orange rind
1 large piece lemon rind
3 oz / 75 ml honey

Combine all the ingredients in a saucepan and heat gently for no more than 10 minutes before serving in heatproof glasses.

This traditional winter drink has made something of a comeback of late, turning up at more Halloween, Guy Fawkes Night, Thanksgiving and Christmas parties than ever before. The mulling of wine goes back as far as Roman times, when the first known instances of wine being heated and spiced were recorded. Since then, countries across Europe have all developed their own twist on the theme. In France, *vin chaud* is a common and simple mix of spices and citrus heated with wine, whereas the Nordic countries make *glögg* with a rich blend of warming spices and often add a spirit such as brandy or vodka to fortify the mix.

• •

Paralysed by the news of Lady Diana's tragic death in Paris, Amélie starts a chain reaction, dropping her perfume stopper which dislodges a tile which reveals a small tin that was hidden in her wall 40 years previously: a perfect little time capsule. As she lies in bed that night, she resolves to find the owner and reunite them with their childhood memories. After visiting several Paris addresses, she fails to find the right Mr Bredoteau. When she returns home a little crestfallen, her reclusive neighbour Mr Dufayel, whom she has never met, offers her invaluable information and the greatest comforter of all – a steaming glass of Mulled Wine.

NEGRONI

The Roman Spring of Mrs Stone • 1962
Karen Stone / Vivien Leigh

1½ oz / 37.5 ml gin
1½ oz / 37.5 ml Campari
1½ oz / 37.5 ml sweet red vermouth

Fill an Old-Fashioned glass with ice, pour all the ingredients in and stir gently. Peel a strip of zest from an orange and fold lengthways while holding over the glass to express the oils into the drink. Finally, twist the zest and place in the drink to garnish.

This distinctive classic was reportedly named after Count Camillo Negroni, who frequented Caffè Casoni in Florence around 1919. He would take his Americano a little differently, requesting that bartender Fosco Scarselli replace the soda water with gin, making for a much stronger drink. In time this drink became a cocktail in its own right and would carry the count's name in honour of what is now perhaps the definitive Italian aperitif. It remains an acquired taste, and a drink that few people fall in love with the first time round. Given time, though, its bitter orange bite and chorus of herbal flavours may become a preprandial favourite.

. . . .

Stage actress Karen Stone has landed in Rome with her husband, who has died from a severe heart attack on the plane. She is comforted by two things: a gigolo named Paolo and the almost constant presence of a Negroni, well iced to counter the rising heat, of course. Who can blame her? The enduring Italian classic is a drink so sophisticated that even when Mrs Stone imbibes it to lift her spirits, she retains the inimitable cygnine elegance on which her illustrious career was built.

OLD FASHIONED

Crazy Stupid Love • 2011
Jacob Palmer / Ryan Gosling

2 oz / 50 ml bourbon
2 dashes Angostura bitters
½ oz / 12.5 ml sugar syrup

Fill an Old-Fashioned glass with ice, pour in the ingredients and stir for at least one minute to allow the mix to cool and dilute properly. If the ice has reduced down slightly, top the glass up with ice. Peel some zest off an orange and fold lengthways over the glass to express the oils. Twist and drop in the glass.

The Old Fashioned first appears in the earliest popular cocktail book, Jerry Thomas's *How to Mix Drinks* from 1862. Here it is listed as a 'Whiskey Cocktail' and the ingredients are the same, except for the non-specific mention of 'whiskey' rather than a named variant such as bourbon or rye, and it is served in a wine glass. Nowadays, of course, this 'vintage cocktail' is served in the thick-bottomed tumblers which took on the drink's name. For a time Old Fashioneds were made with muddled orange, lemon and cherry, and topped with soda water. Thankfully, the Old Fashioned is now usually served in its classic form.

. . . .

Cal's life has crumbled, his marriage has fallen apart and he's just a lonely man with terrible dress sense to boot. Seemingly out of the blue lands his potential saviour, Jacob, the most suave and quietly sexy guy in all of Los Angeles. Here's a man who effortlessly seduces a different woman every night with his cat-like coolness, bottomless well of confidence and, in his hand, a drink that is like a baton passed through the ages between men of sophistication and urbane allure: the Old Fashioned.

ORANGE WHIP

The Blues Brothers • 1980
Burton Mercer / John Candy

4 oz / 100 ml orange juice
1 oz / 25 ml light rum
1 oz / 25 ml vodka
2 oz / 50 ml single (light) cream

Blend all the ingredients and pour into an ice-filled Collins glass.

Prior to its appearance in this film, this drink was not well known, so its history is unclear. Although this scene boosted the cocktail's popularity, its mention in the movie was down to a member of the costume department, Sue Dugan, asking director John Landis if the film could contain a mention of the soft drink company her father worked for, the Orange Whip Corporation. He agreed and John Candy completely improvised the scene after instruction from Landis. It's not known whether it was a favour or paid product placement, but the company is no longer trading and the legacy lives on in the form of this creamy, tall cocktail.

. . . .

Jake and Elwood Blues are on a mission from God to raise the $5,000 needed to save the orphanage they grew up in. Having put their band back together, they've left a trail of destruction, traffic violations and IOUs behind them. Now they've finally landed the gig that could solve all their problems, but the cops, led by Burton Mercer, are waiting in the wings to arrest them. As the Brothers sneak through the venue to get to the stage, Cab Calloway raises the roof with his classic crowd-pleaser 'Minnie the Moocher'. Mercer orders Orange Whips for himself and the police officers, a fine way to refresh oneself in the presence of jazz aristocracy.

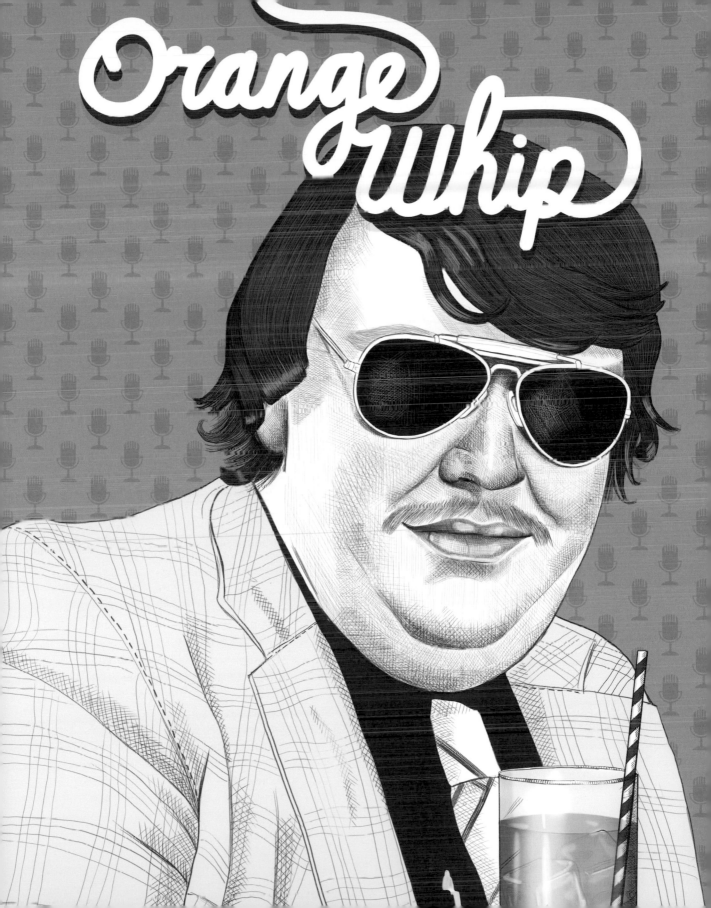

PAN GALACTIC GARGLE BLASTER

The Hitchhiker's Guide to the Galaxy • 2005
Zaphod Beeblebrox / Sam Rockwell

1 oz / 25 ml bourbon
1 oz / 25 ml peach schnapps
4 oz / 100 ml orange juice
½ oz / 12.5 ml blue curaçao

Shake all the ingredients with ice and fine strain into a chilled Martini glass. Garnish with a thin lemon twist.

This fictitious concoction initially appeared in the original radio drama on BBC Radio 4 in 1978, where the people of Earth first heard Douglas Adams's enduring story. It has since been told through a series of novels, television shows, video games, comic books and a film in 2005. Many recipes for it have been created in bars all over the planet, most of which focus on making the drink incredibly (and undrinkably) strong. Here we've opted for an appropriately cosmic-coloured drink, adapted from a recipe said to originate from a Hitchhiker-themed bar, Zaphod Beeblebrox in Ottawa, Canada. It's a candy-sweet drink in which good bourbon contrasts surprisingly well with the peach and orange flavours.

Zaphod Beeblebrox, the former President of the Galaxy, is a man with everything: his own spaceship, two heads, three arms. He also happens to be the inventor of the Pan Galactic Gargle Blaster, the drink which the *Guide* considers the best in existence. Zaphod is the only person alive who can drink more than three in one sitting, and advises all who dare put their lips to it never to drink more than two. The effects are apparently 'similar to having your brains smashed in by a slice of lemon wrapped round a large gold brick'.

RAMOS FIZZ

The Doors • 1991
Jim Morrison / Val Kilmer

2 oz / 50 ml gin
½ oz / 12.5 ml lemon juice
½ oz / 12.5 ml lime juice
¾ oz / 19 ml sugar syrup
3 dashes orange flower water
3 drops vanilla extract
1 egg white
2 oz / 50 ml single (light) cream
Soda water

Dry shake (without ice) all the ingredients except the soda vigorously for one minute, add ice and shake until the outside of the shaker is frosted. Strain into a Collins glass without ice, and top with soda.

The Ramos Gin Fizz is named after its creator, Henry C. Ramos, who invented the drink in 1888 at his bar, Imperial Cabinet Saloon in New Orleans. It is sometimes called the New Orleans Fizz, and originally went by that name, as it quickly became a firm favourite in the Big Easy. This is a drink that takes an uncompromising amount of time to prepare, and at the height of its popularity Ramos's bar would have up to 33 bartenders shaking the drink for the thirsty crowds. The recipe was a well-kept secret until Ramos's death, during Prohibition. In honour of his creation, his brother Charles later published the recipe as a full-page advertisement in the local newspaper to share this great drink with the world.

Having been treated to a backstage spray of mace in the eyes, Jim badmouths the cops on stage at the New Haven Arena, whipping up a riot when he's finally dragged off stage and roughly arrested. Back home in West Hollywood, Jim seeks solace in his local dive bar, Barney's Beanery, where he enjoys a Dos Equis beer to clear the palate and a Ramos Gin Fizz, which he downs with aplomb before relieving himself all over the bar. Not recommended drinking practice if you want to be welcomed back to your favourite cocktail establishment.

ROB ROY

Angels Over Broadway • 1940
Nina Barona / Rita Hayworth

1½ oz / 37.5 ml Scotch whisky
¾ oz / 19 ml sweet vermouth
1 dash orange bitters

Stir all the ingredients with ice and strain into a chilled Martini glass.

The Rob Roy is essentially a Manhattan but with Scotch as the base spirit. It was allegedly created at the Waldorf Astoria in New York to honour the opening of an operetta of the same name, which played at the Herald Square Theatre in October 1894. Older recipes tend to recommend equal measures of vermouth and whisky, with guides from the 1950s onwards advising that half as much vermouth be used. Most recipes call for Angostura bitters, though in *The Old Waldorf Astoria Bar Book* from 1935 orange bitters are used. These are recommended here in consideration of the date of the movie and the likely practices at the drink's birthplace.

• •

Bill, a New York hustler, has spotted an opportunity to make some money in rich businessman Charles Engel, whom he plans to take to a card game and fleece for all he's worth. He needs some feminine charm to ensnare his prey, and ropes beautiful Nina into his cunning plot. As they sip a Rob Roy, the details are worked out. Little do they know, poor old Engel is an embezzler with debts of thousands, and the ensuing poker game might just be the suicidal man's lifeline.

RUM COLLINS

Thunderball • 1965
James Bond / Sean Connery

2 oz / 50 ml light rum
½ oz / 12.5 ml lime juice
½ oz / 12.5 ml sugar syrup
2 dashes Angostura bitters
Soda water

Pour the first four ingredients into an ice-filled Collins glass, stir and top up with the soda before stirring gently. Garnish with a lime wedge.

The Collins has grown from the simple gin drink named after Tom to become a whole family of drinks with a long list of wittily named variants based on the origin of the base spirit. The key ones to know are John Collins (made with bourbon), Comrade Collins (vodka), José Collins (tequila), Pierre Collins (brandy), Mike Collins (Irish whiskey) and Pedro Collins, which, as detailed here, is made with light rum.

After nearly being killed scuba diving under supervillain Largo's yacht, Bond is safely ashore and finds himself in the company of a delightful Bahamian, the flame-haired Fiona. He has the intelligence he needs but wants to meet Largo face-to-face in his home. As he calmly strolls into the SPECTRE operative's Caribbean lair, Bond is offered a Rum Collins and a tour of the patio, along with its pool of notoriously savage golden grotto sharks. Little does he know he'll be sharing their watery domain before long, and only his trademark gadgets can save him.

SANGRIA

Legally Blonde 2 • 2003
Elle Woods / Reese Witherspoon

3 oz / 75 ml red wine
½ oz / 12.5 ml brandy
1 oz / 25 ml orange juice
½ oz / 12.5 ml lemon juice
½ oz / 12.5 ml sugar syrup
Soda water

In this single-serving version, simply build the drink in an ice-filled Hurricane glass, top up with soda and stir gently. Dust with grated nutmeg and garnish with an orange slice.

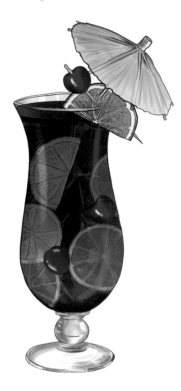

Sangria, or Sangaree as it is often called in older mixology guides, is a Spanish drink that was first recorded in its modern form in the early 18th century. As a general type of drink it is likely to be much older, potentially as old as wine production itself. It is simply red wine fortified on the spot, perhaps to improve a poor-quality vino or just to make a more interesting and cooling drink. Its name derives from the Spanish for blood (*sangre*) due to its visceral range of crimsons, particularly when served long over ice.

· ·

Elle Woods is on a mission to change laws on animal testing. She goes to Washington, DC, to get her 'Bruiser Bill' considered by Congress, but must first survive a committee hearing with her new legal partner. No-one in the District has yet had time to get used to a lawyer who wears so much hot pink, and carries an immaculately dressed Chihuahua to boot. Elle is, ambitiously, already planning her 'post-hopper toppers' party to celebrate submitting her Bill to Congress and is making sangria, which she assures the committee is 'really yummy'.

SAZERAC

Live and Let Die • 1973
James Bond / Roger Moore

1 oz / 25 ml absinthe
2 oz / 50 ml rye whiskey
½ oz / 12.5 ml sugar syrup
2 dashes Peychaud's bitters

Rinse a chilled Old-Fashioned glass with absinthe, fill it with crushed ice and put it in the fridge to cool further. Stir the other ingredients with ice and strain into your (emptied) ice-chilled glass. Twist a piece of lemon zest over the drink and drop it in.

The Sazerac is the drink most closely associated with New Orleans. Its name comes from a French cognac, Sazerac-de-Forge et Fils, which Aaron Bird started importing to the city in around 1850. Bird opened the Sazerac Coffee House and combined the cognac with locally made Peychaud's bitters. Around 1870, cognac became scarce due to the epidemic of phylloxera, a parasite from America that had accidentally been imported and decimated European vineyards. As a result rye whiskey was used instead. It remains the most popular base spirit. In 2008 the cocktail was proclaimed the official drink of the Big Easy.

• •

Bond is in New Orleans to track down the killer of a number of British MI6 agents. He's on the trail of Caribbean dictator Kananga with CIA agent Felix. The pair go to Fillet of Soul for some local seafood and, of course, the local tipple, Sazeracs. Unfortunately, it transpires that the place is owned by local gangster Mr Big. Bond is left alone at the table for a moment and it descends into the floor just before the drinks arrive, offering him an impromptu meeting with the boss and his unexpected alter ego.

SCOTCH MIST

The Big Sleep • 1946
Vivian Rutledge / Lauren Bacall

2 oz / 50 ml Scotch whisky
Crushed ice
Lemon peel

Pack an Old-Fashioned glass with crushed ice. Pour in the Scotch, twist a strip of lemon zest over the drink and drop it in.

This simple drink is like an adult snow cone in which whisky is sipped ice-cold and diluted quickly by the finely crushed ice. Only the twist of lemon adds some flavour, which is highly complementary and rounds off the pure alcohol aroma of the whisky. Your choice of whisky is paramount with this, as it is with Old Fashioneds and the like, as there's little room for a low-quality spirit to hide.

Philip Marlowe, a Los Angeles private investigator, has been tasked with looking after a wealthy general's daughter. Carmen and her father are being blackmailed. As the web of deceit, extortion and murder starts to get bigger and more complex, Marlowe finds it hard to keep his mind on the job. The general's other daughter, Vivian, is both beautiful and seductive, and over a cool Scotch Mist Marlowe realizes he's falling for her.

SCREWDRIVER

Jackie Brown • 1997
Ordell Robbie / Samuel L. Jackson

2 oz / 50 ml vodka
Orange juice

Pour the vodka into an ice-filled Old-Fashioned glass, top up with orange juice and stir gently.

A very rudimentary Highball drink with a million variations, the Screwdriver seems to have come about in the 1930s through the marketing efforts of Smirnoff, though there are more interesting origin stories from the mid-century. They mostly involve American aviators, oil riggers and GIs posted to exotic places who mixed their juice with vodka and stirred it with their screwdrivers, but these tales seem unlikely. Some of the more notable variants of the drink include the Sloe Screw (with sloe gin), Comfortable Screw (Southern Comfort), Royal Screw (Chambord), Double Screw (triple sec) and Harvey Wallbanger (vodka and Galliano).

It's a hot California afternoon in Hermosa Beach, and Ordell Robbie, a black-market arms dealer, is enjoying hanging with his buddy Louis. They're lazing on the couch watching his favourite video, *Chicks Who Love Guns*, an unlikely juxtaposition but an entertaining watch for fans of the latest assault rifles and semi-automatic pistols. As they drool over beautiful babes with destructive tendencies, the drinks must be kept iced, particularly Ordell's signature Screwdriver.

SEA BREEZE

French Kiss • 1995
Kate / Meg Ryan

2 oz / 50 ml vodka
6 oz / 150 ml cranberry juice
1½ oz / 37.5 ml grapefruit juice

Pour the ingredients into an ice-filled Highball glass and stir gently. Garnish with a lime wedge.

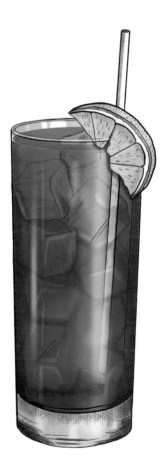

The Sea Breeze first appeared during the 1920s in America, but it has changed significantly since then. In the *Café Royal Cocktail Book* by W. J. Tarling, published the year following Prohibition's repeal in 1933, it is described as containing gin, apricot brandy, grenadine and lemon juice. It may not have been sufficiently popular to become widely known. Cranberry-juice marketing efforts in the 1950s created the Cape Codder, a variant of which successfully appropriated the Sea Breeze name and consigned the original to history.

. . . .

Kate's come all the way from Canada to France to win back her ex-fiancé, Charlie. He's fallen for a French beauty and called off their wedding. When she finally catches up with him on the beach in Cannes, she plays it cool and orders a tall, icy Sea Breeze. As she sips, she introduces her own Gallic 'fling', Luc, a conman who is only there to make Charlie jealous. But as Kate plays out the charade of having moved on and found love herself, she starts to believe her own fiction.

SEX ON THE BEACH

Hysterical Blindness • 2002
Beth / Juliette Lewis

2 oz / 50 ml vodka
½ oz / 12.5 ml peach schnapps
1½ oz / 37.5 ml orange juice
1½ oz / 37.5 ml cranberry juice

Combine the ingredients in an ice-filled Highball glass and stir, or layer gently for a colour gradation effect. Garnish with an orange slice and serve with long straws.

The quintessential 1980s drink was reportedly born in Florida in 1987 when National Distribution offered $1,000 to the bar that could sell the most of their latest product line, peach schnapps, with $100 for the barman too. Ted Pizio, a bartender at Confetti's in Fort Lauderdale, Florida, took up the challenge and created this drink, naming it after the two things that people flock to his town for during Spring Break. The drink became popular fast, with tourists returning home and ordering it at bars all over the world, much to the initial bemusement of their local bartenders. It thus had many variations, both intentional and not.

. . . .

Debby and Beth are looking for love, and somehow think they'll find it in local dive bar Ollie's. They agree over makeup and hairspray in the ladies' toilets that tonight starts with tequila shots with salt, before moving on to bottles of beer. They leave the restroom full of poise and confidence, take a seat at the bar and wait for Bobby to come over. He clearly likes Beth more, and she gets excited, ordering a Sex on the Beach instead of tequila and beer. Debby can't believe that Beth reneged on their washroom deal, and knows that Beth was just flirting anyway. It is, after all, almost impossible not to flirt when ordering this drink.

SINGAPORE SLING

Fear and Loathing in Las Vegas • 1998
Raoul Duke / Johnny Depp

1½ oz / 37.5 ml gin
½ oz / 12.5 ml cherry brandy
¼ oz / 6 ml Cointreau
¼ oz / 6 ml DOM Bénédictine
⅓ oz / 8 ml grenadine
3 oz / 75 ml pineapple juice
1 oz / 25 ml fresh lemon juice
1 dash Angostura bitters

Shake all the ingredients with ice and pour into an ice-filled Sling glass. Garnish with a pineapple slice and a Maraschino cherry. Side of mescal optional.

Originating from the Long Bar at Singapore's Raffles Hotel, this Sling was an early 20th-century take on the Gin Slings of America, which dated from the 18th century and were described as 'a drink of gin flavoured, sweetened and served cold'. In 1915 Singapore had been a British colony for almost 100 years. In this tasty concoction, Raffles bartender Ngiam Tong Boon combined the colonial powers of Europe in a monsoon of flavours: gin and grenadine from Britain or Holland, Cherry Heering liqueur from Denmark, Cointreau and Benedictine from France, Angostura bitters from Germany and juice from the tropics.

. . . .

The patio of the Polo Lounge at the Beverly Hills Hotel is where Raoul and Gonzo's mind-bending journey into the desert begins. After drinking a table full of Singapore Slings, with a tequila-like spirit called mescal on the side, Raoul takes a call on the bar's bright pink telephone, and with it their directive to head to Las Vegas to cover the Mint 400 motorcycle race. Sounds like a simple job, but their car full of booze and hallucinogens has other ideas.

STINGER

Beaches • 1988
CC Bloom / Bette Midler

2 oz / 50 ml cognac
¾ oz / 19 ml white crème de menthe

Stir the ingredients in a stirring or mixing glass with ice for about 30 seconds, then strain into a chilled California cocktail glass.

The Stinger has waned in popularity in recent years. In the mid-20th century it was referenced in films and songs regularly as a nightcap as well as a hangover cure. It's one of those drinks that gives the impression of being medicinal, with the burn of the brandy and cleansing cool of the mint. Since its inception sometime in the 1910s, it has been modified, with the crème de menthe content coming down to make a much less mouthwash-esque drink. There are now also numerous variants. Use green crème de menthe to make a Grasshopper or try vodka instead of brandy for a Vodka Stinger.

· ·

The club is barely populated, but CC sings her heart out anyway, just like she does every night. Her infinite optimism shines through, and she's high on the adoration of the handful of punters. Treating herself to her favourite drink of all, the Stinger, she relaxes at the bar. A tall brunette lady walks in, with a big smile and eyes just for CC. She says she's dreamed about this moment for so long. Is she an admirer? Her stalker? It's Hilary! Her childhood friend, bringing the possibility of new adventures ready to unfold before them.

STOLI MARTINI WITH A TWIST

Blue Jasmine • 2013
Jasmine French / Cate Blanchett

2 oz / 50 ml vodka
½ oz / 12.5 ml dry vermouth
1 strip lemon zest

Stir the ingredients in a stirring or mixing glass with ice for about 30 seconds, then strain into a chilled Martini glass. Peel a strip of zest from a lemon, fold it lengthways over the drink to express the oils, wipe it around the rim of the glass, twist it and drop it into the drink.

A Vodka Martini simply replaces the traditional base spirit of gin with vodka for an equally punchy little drink. The first mention of this variant appears in Ted Saucier's 1951 book *Bottoms Up*. While it was one of James Bond's favourite tipples, it is distinct from the Vesper Martini that Bond's creator Ian Fleming famously invented in *Casino Royale*, which uses a specific blend of gin, vodka and aperitif wine. As the vodka here is such a key ingredient, you may wish to try different brands, and certainly use a good-quality one. Jasmine is clearly partial to Stolichnaya, ordering her cocktail by the Russian producer's commonly known name, 'Stoli'.

. . . .

Jasmine can't help but emotionally unload onto her fellow plane passenger. On and on she babbles, about her husband, about how amazing her life was. The exotic vacations, the passionate love life. And now she's left with neuroses and anxieties she can't control. The doctors just prescribe her medication, and lots of it. They call it a cocktail but she says there's only one cocktail that really helps: a Stoli Martini.

Stoli Martini with a Twist

SWEET VERMOUTH ON THE ROCKS WITH A TWIST

Groundhog Day • 1993
Phil Connors / Bill Murray

2 oz / 50 ml sweet vermouth
1 lemon twist

Fill a rocks glass with ice. Pour the vermouth over the ice. Peel a strip of zest off a lemon. Twist this over the drink to express the oils and plunge the twisted peel into the glass as a garnish. Serve with a cocktail straw.

Sweet vermouth in its current form originated in 18th-century Turin. It was popularized by Cinzano and other makers as a fashionable aperitif across Europe. The drink's name reveals a centuries-long heritage of medicinal and fortified wines in medieval Europe and across ancient Asia, traditionally including wormwood, or in German *Wermut*. Vermouth, sweet or dry, is a distilled blend of wine, sugar, alcohol and various botanicals: roots, barks, flowers, seeds, herbs and spices. Modern manufacturers don't reveal their exact recipes, but rather leave us to wonder at their complex depths of flavour.

•••••••••••••••••••••••••••••••••••••

TV weatherman Phil is reporting from Punxsutawney, home of the annual Groundhog Day celebrations, and after being snowed in to the small town becomes inexplicably caught in an infinitely looping 24 hours. He soon realizes he can use his knowledge of this perpetual day to his advantage. In an attempt to get closer to his producer, Rita, he orders her favourite drink at the bar and raises his glass to her usual toast – world peace. How can she resist such 'chemistry'?

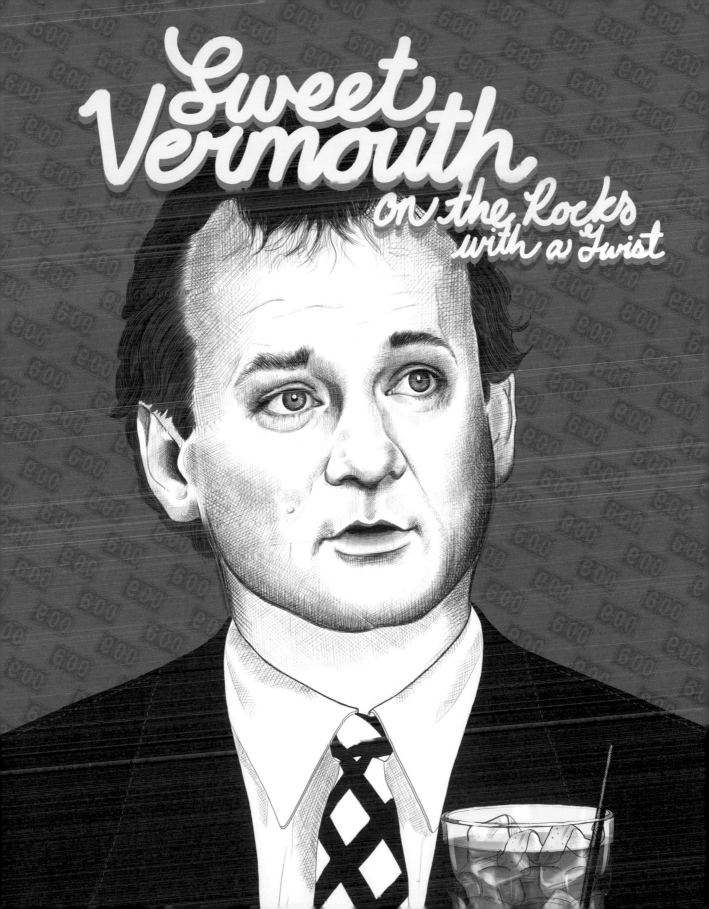

TEQUILA SUNRISE

Tequila Sunrise • 1988
Dale 'Mac' McKussic / Mel Gibson

2 oz / 50 ml tequila
Orange juice
⅔ oz / 17 ml grenadine

Pour the tequila into an ice-filled Highball glass and top up with orange juice. Stir gently before drizzling the grenadine onto the drink, which will sink to create a sunrise effect. Garnish with an orange slice skewered on a stick with a cherry.

The Arizona Biltmore Hotel in Phoenix is the birthplace of this classic. Sometime around 1940 a regular at the bar allegedly asked Gene Sulit for something refreshing and surprising, to which he responded with the original crème de cassis version of the drink. The modern recipe with grenadine was created in the early 1970s in northern California by Bobby Lazoff and Billy Rice at the Trident. Keith Richards recounts in his autobiography how Mick Jagger tried the drink there in 1972 while The Rolling Stones were on tour in America. The whole entourage got to drinking them and continued to do so throughout the tour, which they would jokingly dub the 'cocaine and Tequila Sunrise tour'.

. . . .

Being a big-time drug dealer trying to go straight isn't easy. Everyone assumes you're up to no good, including friends. 'Mac' McKussic is just trying to have dinner in peace at a local restaurant, but his pal Nick just made lieutenant in the Los Angeles Police Department, and is duty-bound to question his friend's current movements. Over his Italian dinner, Mac protests his innocence, though there seem to be more important things on his mind anyway. The owner of this restaurant, a beautiful blonde who serves him long Tequila Sunrises, is growing on him.

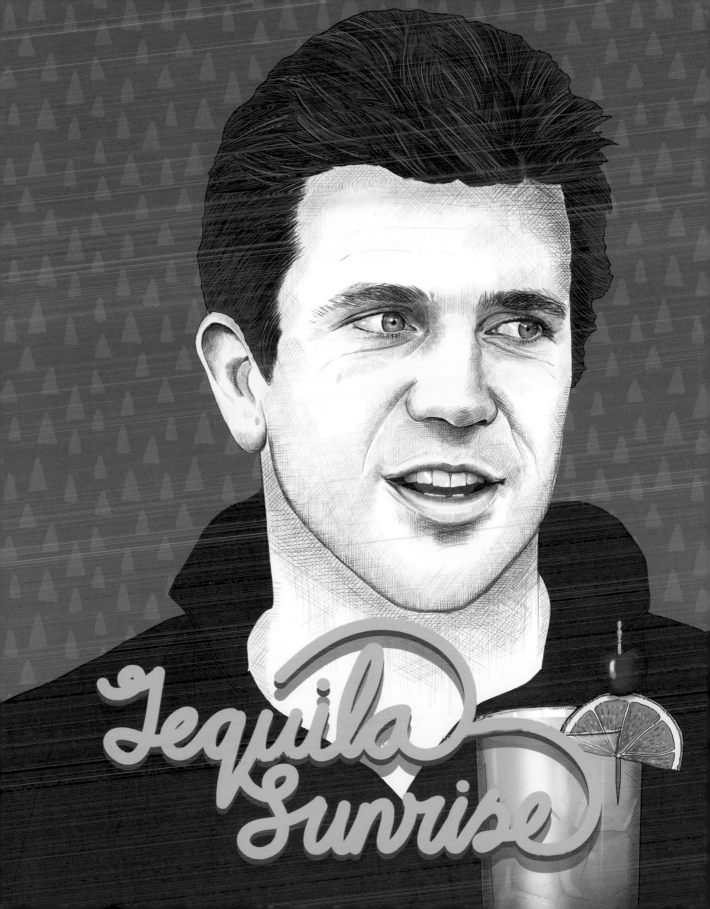

TOM COLLINS

Meet the Parents • 2000
Jack Byrnes / Robert De Niro

2 oz / 50 ml London gin
1 oz / 25 ml freshly squeezed lemon juice
½ oz / 12.5 ml sugar syrup
Soda water

Mix the gin, lemon juice and sugar syrup in a Collins glass with ice, top up with soda and garnish with a lemon slice and a Maraschino cherry.

The Tom Collins is from the genesis era of cocktails. Its origin lies in the heady days of the early 1800s, though historians still disagree over which side of the Atlantic it was born on. If it is American, it was named after the Tom Collins Hoax of 1874, a contagious joke in which New Yorkers would ask after a fictitious Tom Collins, claiming that he had been saying things about you. If British, the drink may have originated from a bartender called John Collins at Limmers Old House in Mayfair, London. This most minimal of drinks represents the essence of mixology, containing the core elements of almost every cocktail – spirit, sour and sweet – with the addition of soda to create a tall, refreshing drink.

Jack Byrnes is the world's most suspicious father. When his daughter and her boyfriend arrive at the family home so Greg can ask for Pam's hand in marriage, Jack welcomes them with his favourite drink, a Tom Collins. Then, Greg explains that he's a nurse, a male nurse. It's clear that Jack doesn't quite understand his potential son-in-law's career choice, yet for all his attachment to traditional values he showcases his very modern invention, a hidden surveillance camera system. He assures Greg, 'We'll be watching you.'

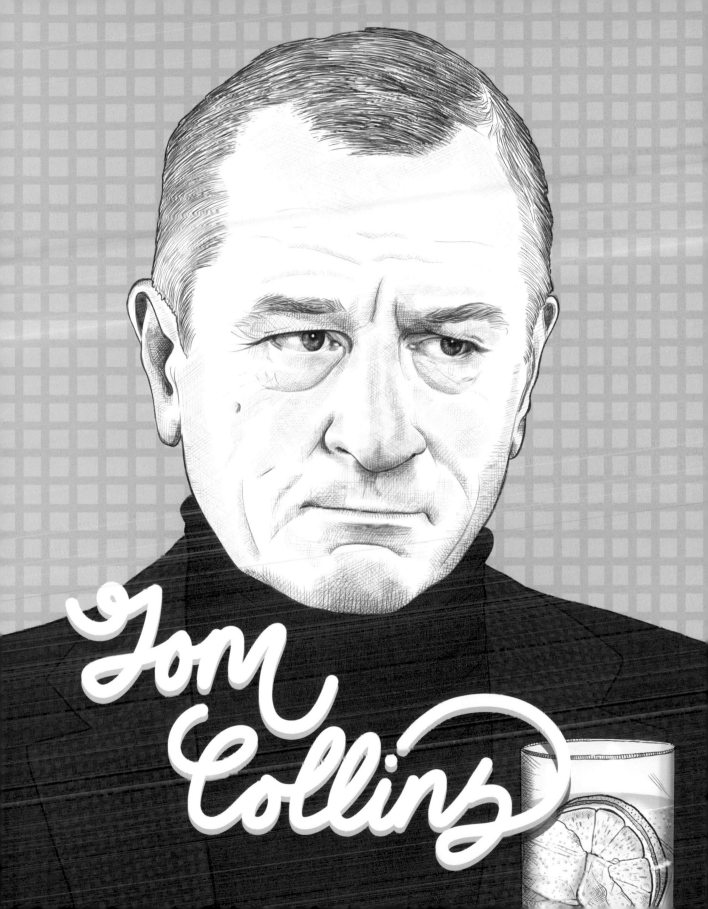

Tom Collins

TURQUOISE BLUE

Cocktail • 1988
Brian Flanagan / Tom Cruise

1 oz / 25 ml light rum
½ oz / 12.5 ml triple sec
½ oz / 12.5 ml blue curaçao
1 oz / 25 ml lime juice
1½ oz / 37.5 ml pineapple juice

Shake all the ingredients with ice and strain into a chilled Martini glass. Serve with a short cocktail straw.

The cocktail known today as a Turquoise Blue likely started life in the hit movie *Cocktail*. Before that notable appearance in the 1988 film, it was known as a Turquoise Daiquiri, and was quite simply a bluer and sweeter variation of the Cuban classic. Indeed, the Daiquiri is a highly adaptable drink. Its core ingredients of lime juice, light rum and sugar welcome the addition of a myriad of flavours from almond to ylang-ylang, and anything in between which your imagination can lead you to experiment with.

The flair and charisma of bartenders Douglas and Brian have drawn the attention of the owner of Cell Block, the hottest bar in town. He insists they come and work for him instead of being wasted in this 'hole'. Their new gig sees them drawing a large, rapturous audience of yuppies, fashionistas and trendsetters. After an impassioned bit of improvised poetry atop the bar, Brian is asked for an Orgasm by Coral, a photographer for *Rolling Stone*. He suggests she starts with a Turquoise Blue and so his choreographed flairing with Douglas begins, to make the bright blue drink just for her. Perhaps he serves her original order later that night when invited to her apartment.

VIRGIN PIÑA COLADA

Death Proof • 2007
Stuntman Mike / Kurt Russell

6 oz / 150 ml pineapple juice
2 oz / 50 ml coconut cream
1 oz / 25 ml single (light) cream

Blend all the ingredients with a cup of crushed ice, then serve in a chilled Hurricane glass. Garnish with a pineapple wedge and a cocktail cherry on a skewer. Replace the cream with 2 oz / 50 ml light rum for the original version of this cocktail.

The national drink of Puerto Rico is a creamy delight whose history is disputed. While the Barrachina Restaurant in San Juan proudly displays a plaque commemorating its creation in 1963, two bartenders at the island's Hilton hotel bar claim to have invented it 11 years earlier. We'll never really know. The drink doesn't appear in books until the late 1960s, though there is a mention in a 1922 travel magazine of a Cuban drink by the same name, described as 'the juice of a perfectly ripe pineapple, rapidly shaken up with ice, sugar, lime and Bacardi rum'. Given the combination of popular local ingredients, it may well be that all the origin stories are true in their own way.

As he sits at the bar eating nachos, Stuntman Mike gets talking to Pam, a pretty blonde with attitude. She buys him a Virgin Piña Colada and the couple get chatting. Stuntman Mike's been in plenty of TV shows and movies, though Pam and the other drinkers in the bar haven't heard of a single one of them. So he goes outside and receives his promised lap dance from sultry Arlene. As Stuntman Mike himself says, he doesn't come to the bar for the alcohol; that's just a social lubricant. He comes for two things only: women and nachos.

VODKA GIMLET

About Schmidt • 2002
Warren Schmidt / Jack Nicholson

2 oz / 50 ml vodka
½ oz / 12.5 ml lime cordial

Shake the ingredients with ice and strain into a chilled Martini glass. Garnish with a lime wheel mounted on the rim.

This drink allegedly has its origins in the British Navy, courtesy of Rear-Admiral Sir Thomas Desmond Gimlette, a naval doctor. Legend has it that, while in service at the end of the 19th century, he gave the sailors gin mixed with lime cordial. This was his way of promoting the consumption of scurvy-preventing citrus fruit. Rose's lime cordial, which has been produced since 1868, is closely tied with the drink's history and has always been specified as the second ingredient. The substitution of gin with vodka is a recent development and makes for a much more pure lime drink, without the complex botanical flavours of gin.

Warren Schmidt was a great man of Omaha, with a career in insurance spanning decades. His retirement dinner is attended by many and he is showered with love and respect, yet he feels the purpose being extracted from his life like the filling from a sandwich. What will he be left with? A lifelong friend delivers an impassioned speech about the riches of the soul that a man like Schmidt can enjoy, having lived a life of virtue and purpose. Warren retreats from the party to the bar for a Vodka Gimlet and a moment of solace, to reflect on life and the road ahead.

VODKA 'VESPER' MARTINI

Casino Royale • 2006
James Bond / Daniel Craig

2 oz / 50 ml gin
½ oz / 12.5 ml vodka
¼ oz / 6 ml Lillet Blonde

Shake all the ingredients with ice and strain into a chilled Martini glass. Garnish with a large, thin strip of lemon zest.

This may be the only well-known drink invented by a fictional character. In the novel *Casino Royale*, James Bond is in the casino and orders a Dry Martini before giving very specific orders on the recipe and preparation, which of course includes shaking. This scene has since been depicted faithfully in the movie of the same name, including the reference to Kina Lillet, a drink that no longer exists. The Lillet company still makes its replacement, a similar but more mellow white-wine-based aperitif.

James has entered the biggest poker game of his life. With hundreds of millions on the table, he needs to win to bankrupt Le Chiffre, a private banker and financier to terrorists. The game goes on over days, and the tension is rising with the stakes. Bond asks the barman to come over and orders a Dry Martini, though with his own heavy customization. His fellow players like the sound of this punchy-sounding drink and his creation starts to catch on. As he sips thoughtfully, he looks to the demure Vesper, a fellow agent and lover, and ponders how he might christen this new drink.

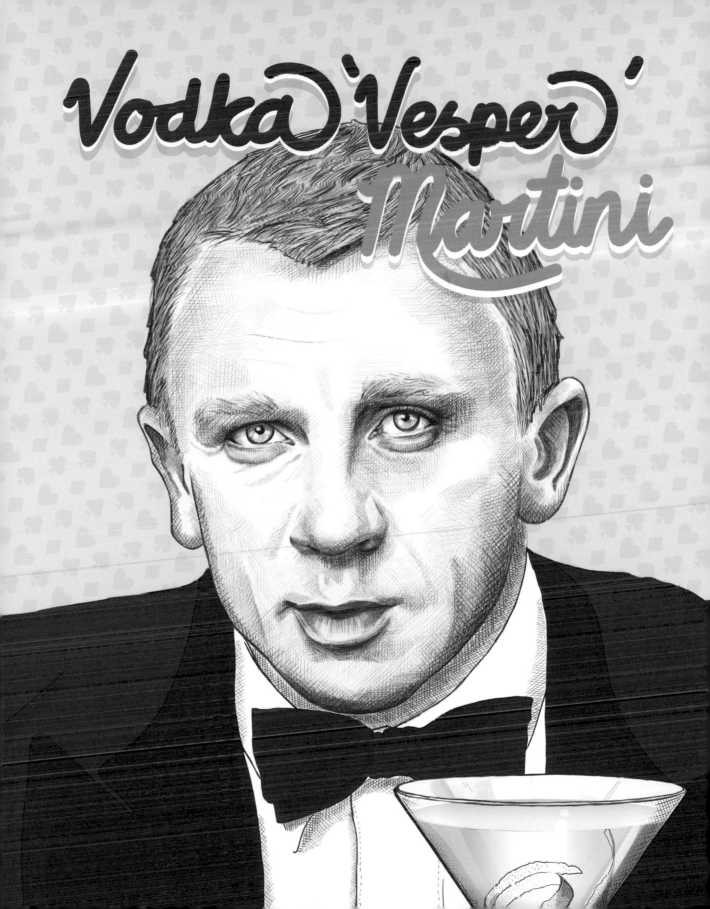

WHISKEY SOUR

Avanti! • 1972
Wendell Armbruster, Jr. / Jack Lemmon

2 oz / 50 ml bourbon
1 oz / 25 ml lemon juice
½ oz / 12.5 ml sugar syrup
2 dashes Angostura bitters
½ an egg white

Shake all the ingredients with ice and strain into a chilled champagne flute. Garnish with an orange slice.

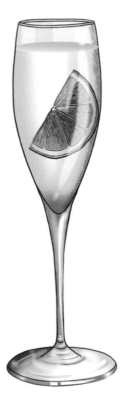

Mentions of this drink can be found as early as 1870, and it has since become a whole family of cocktails. Some recipes, such as David A. Embury's 8:2:1 formula in the 1954 edition of *The Fine Art of Mixing Drinks*, dial up the whiskey ratio, whereas more modern bartenders will likely serve it as we describe here, with more lemon and sugar. This drink works equally well whether served straight up or on the rocks. Irish or rye whiskey step in happily in place of bourbon, but never Scotch. Its peat flavours don't work well with lemon.

....

Wendell's trying his best to navigate Italian red tape and corruption, and all he wants is to retrieve the body of his recently deceased father. The old man died as his car careered off a winding road in the Neapolitan countryside. What Wendell doesn't know is that his father died alongside his mistress of ten years, which explains why Wendell bumps into Pamela, an English woman who has come to Italy to retrieve her own mother's body. The pair decide to honour their parents' memories by doing the very same things they loved to do, checking out the restaurants, hotels and sights. At the Hotel Excelsior, the barman serves exactly what their parents would have had: a Whiskey Sour, on the sour side, and a Bacardi, on the sweet side.

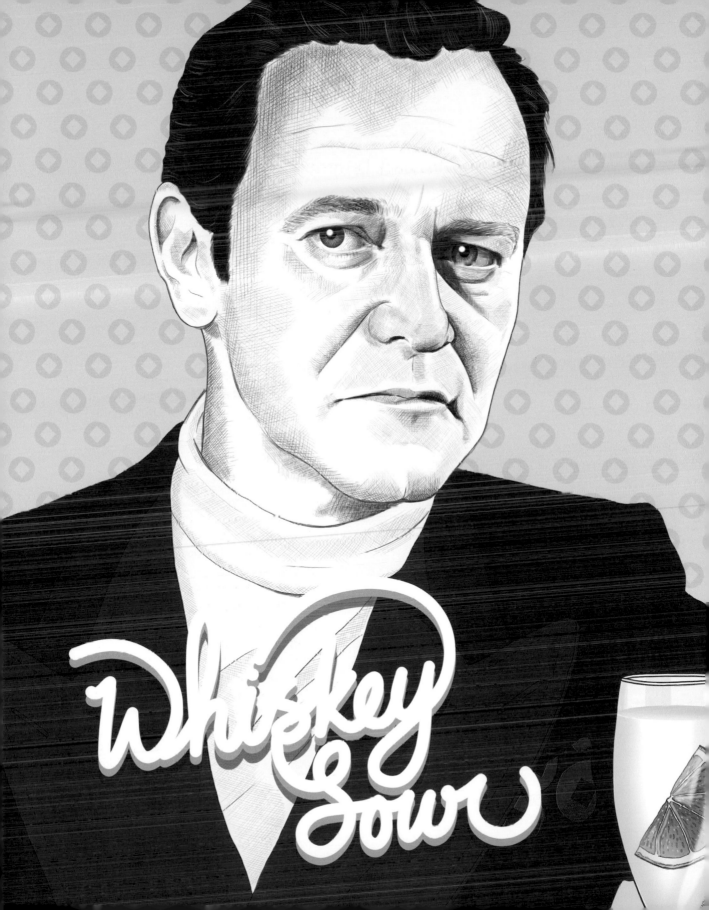

WHITE LADY

Evil Under the Sun • 1982
Hercule Poirot / Peter Ustinov

1⅓ oz / 33 ml gin
1 oz / 25 ml triple sec
¾ oz / 19 ml lemon juice

Shake all the ingredients with ice and strain into a chilled Martini glass.

This cocktail has an origin story that is caught in a tug of war between two titans of mixology history. Harry MacElhone claims he created it at Ciro's Club, London, in 1919. He apparently went on to refine the recipe to the one we now know in 1929 while running the legendary Harry's Bar in Paris. However, in the 1930 *Savoy Cocktail Book*, Harry Craddock includes the cocktail, claiming it as his own. Harry's former apprentice, Joe Gilmore, backs the claim and remembers it as the favourite drink of Laurel and Hardy.

· ·

Poirot's latest assignment finds him on the idyllic island resort of Tyrania, following the trail of a fake diamond. The Belgian sleuth fancies that he'll be able to enjoy a little time out for himself while tracking down the jewel, and attends the host's canapé and cocktail welcome party. There he meets his fellow guests, an eclectic bunch of wealthy, creative types. As Hercule is presented with a tempting choice of White Lady, Sidecar, Mainrace or Between the Sheets, he is blissfully unaware that among the guests is a murderer. Will he find out who it is?

WHITE RUSSIAN

The Big Lebowski • 1998
The Dude / Jeff Bridges

2 oz / 50 ml vodka
1 oz / 25 ml coffee liqueur
1 oz / 25 ml single (light) cream

Pour the first two ingredients into an ice-filled Old-Fashioned glass and stir. Float the cream on top by pouring gently over the back of a bar spoon.

One of the newer drinks in this book, the White Russian originated in mid-1960s America, though its creator is unknown. It is a variation on the Black Russian, a drink from the 1940s, with the addition of cream. While the drink was popular in the 1960s and 1970s, its consumption declined until 1998, when this modern classic was thankfully revived. The Dude made it cool again, drinking seven of them with his inimitable nonchalance throughout *The Big Lebowski*. It is now a commonly ordered cocktail, and has variations ranging from the Dirty Russian (with chocolate milk instead of cream) to the White Cuban (rum instead of vodka).

• •

That rug really tied the room together, and now some mistaken thug's pee is all over it. The Dude goes to the man those hoodlums were really looking for, Jeffrey Lebowski, to get some compensation. Despite the old man's lack of sympathy, The Dude manages to make it out of his mansion with a beautiful Persian rug. Back at his ramshackle apartment, he slowly paces triumphantly over his new centrepiece to fix himself a drink. He generously pours vodka, Kahlua and cream over ice to make his favourite drink, a White Russian. As he slurps through his ample moustache, the phone rings. It's Lebowski. He doesn't want his rug back, he just needs The Dude's help.

ZOMBIE

To Gillian on Her 37th Birthday • 1996
Rachel Lewis / Claire Danes

½ oz / 12.5 ml white rum
1½ oz / 37.5 ml golden rum
1 oz / 25 ml dark rum
1 oz / 25 ml lime juice
¾ oz / 19 ml pineapple juice
½ oz / 12.5 ml sugar syrup
½ oz / 12.5 ml apricot liqueur
½ oz / 12.5 ml 151-proof rum

Shake all the ingredients except the 151-proof rum with ice. Strain into a Hurricane glass filled with crushed ice and over the top float the overproof rum, which can be set alight should you desire some theatre in your presentation. Garnish with a pineapple slice.

This is a strong drink that requires you to have four rums in stock, though you can omit the 151-proof rum, as this adds little more than ignitability. Credit for its creation lies with tiki legend Donn Beach, who opened a chain of Polynesian-style restaurants across America, starting the tiki craze of the mid-20th century. His recipe for this drink, as with other creations, remained a secret until later. He would often tweak the recipes, leaving us to guess the exact original formula. One thing we do know is that he'd only serve you two. His restaurants to this day still have a 'two per customer' limit due to the drink's unusual strength.

· ·

It's been two years since Gillian fell from the mast of their sailing ship to her untimely death. David still isn't over it and sees his wife everywhere, holding imaginary conversations with her that are very real to him. Meanwhile, the couple's daughter Rachel is coming of age and being influenced by friends who like to have fun. She accepts an invite to go to a party, where the drink of the night is a heavily loaded Zombie served in plastic pint glasses and with plenty of rum. It's no wonder she ends the night puking on her father's feet!

ACKNOWLEDGEMENTS

. . . .

Making *Cocktails of the Movies* and getting it onto shelves was a long process that began with a thought: 'There should be a book about this.' Thank you to all our friends who told us the idea was worth pursuing. In exploring and pitching the idea to publishers, thank you to all the editors who came back and told us that, even if it wasn't for them, they loved the idea, and in some cases put time into writing comprehensive feedback.

Thanks to our parents for being so proud and turning us into dreamers in the first place.

Thanks to Ali Gitlow at Prestel for believing in this book and championing us.

In researching this book we turned to a million sources of varying reliability and veracity. Some authors stand out as providers of unparalleled authority in the world of mixology. We can highly recommend David A. Embury's *The Fine Art of Mixing Drinks* (1948), Simon Difford's *Diffordsguide* (updated regularly), Patrick Gavin Duffy's *The Official Mixer's Manual* (1934), Harry MacElhone's *ABC of Mixing Cocktails* (1919), Harry Johnson's *Bartender's Manual* (1882) and the first book of this kind, Jerry Thomas's *Bartender's Guide* (1862).

Most of all, at the risk of sounding glib, eternal thanks to each other for unwavering support in the face of deadlines and the creative pressure of producing this book. We're so excited with the result and can't think of a better way to crown the year of our marriage.

. . . .

ABOUT THE AUTHORS

Will Francis is a presenter, writer and commentator on the ever-changing landscape of technology and how it shapes the world in which we live. Formerly UK Editor of the pioneering social network and entertainment site MySpace, Will is now a director of a creative digital agency in London. He regularly appears on TV, radio and in the press to share his expertise and views on social media and digital technology.

WILLFRANCIS.COM

Stacey Marsh is an illustrator and graphic designer originally from Waterford in southeast Ireland. Having worked in London for the last 10 years, Stacey's client list includes a vast array of household brands as well as smaller private commissions. Her work has adorned shop windows and retail spaces, websites and billboards. Stacey is currently launching a range of homeware and fashion bearing her signature style of surreal and colourful patterns.

STACEYMARSH.COM

Will and Stacey live in London. Together they have spent years enjoying some of the finest cocktail bars and cinemas in the world, right on their doorstep. This book was borne out of that shared love of mixology and film, and their dream of crafting a beautiful book together.

Prestel Verlag, Munich
A member of Verlagsgruppe Random House GmbH

Prestel Verlag
Neumarkter Strasse 28
81673 Munich
Tel. +49 (0)89 4136-0
Fax +49 (0)89 4136-2335

www.prestel.de

Prestel Publishing Ltd.
14-17 Wells Street
London W1T 3PD
Tel. +44 (0)20 7323-5004
Fax +44 (0)20 7323-0271

Prestel Publishing
900 Broadway, Suite 603
New York, NY 10003
Tel. +1 (212) 995-2720
Fax +1 (212) 995-2733

www.prestel.com

. . . .

Library of Congress Control Number: 2015936428

British Library Cataloguing-in-Publication Data:
a catalogue record for this book is available from the British Library; Deutsche Nationalbibliothek
holds a record of this publication in the Deutsche Nationalbibliografie; detailed bibliographical
data can be found under: http://dnb.d-nb.de

Prestel books are available worldwide. Please contact your nearest bookseller or one of the
above addresses for information concerning your local distributor.

Editorial direction: Ali Gitlow
Copyediting: Martha Jay
Design and layout: Stacey Marsh
Production: Friederike Schirge
Origination: Reproline Mediateam, Munich
Printing and binding: Neografia a.s.

Printed in Slovakia

ISBN 978-3-7913-8174-9

Verlagsgrupp Random House FSC® N001967
The FSC®-certified paper Profibulk
has been supplied by Igepa, Germany